The Big and Small of God
40 Short Daily Devotionals on Nature's Miracles

the Big & Small of God

of

40 Short Daily Devotionals on Nature's Miracles

by Tonia Davidson
illustrations by Kory Davidson

ISBN: 9798565124194

Cover design and interior illustrations by Kory Davidson

To the three A's—We love you!

Table of Contents:

Introduction

Little 'm' miracles versus capital 'M' miracles

Recently I was reminded of the difference between miracles with a little "m" and miracles with a capital "M". As I sat with the difference, it dawned on me that most of life must be peppered—if not covered—with these little "m" miracles. I couldn't help but feel regret for not taking better notice. I confess that I'm eager to receive God's rescue from difficult circumstances, and I often feel gravely disappointed or mistakenly assume God's impotence with a situation when my struggling circumstances aren't greatly altered.

Don't get me wrong. Big "M" miracles exist. I've witnessed a few. The most staggering was my mother-in-law's cure from macular degeneration. The day the DMV denied her a driver's license, she arrived on our doorstep asking for a prayer. She must have been desperate because she was more apt to put her faith in crystals than God.

It was an odd prayer from the beginning. I'm generally flooded with words when we pray, but not this time. My husband gently placed his hands on his mother's shoulders, while my three young daughters participated by putting their hands on their grandmother's back. As I sat there with my eyes closed, I just kept envisioning Jesus standing in front of my mother-in-law, his hands passing through her eye sockets. I felt a nagging tug that I was supposed to stand in front of her and put my hands on her eyes. We were not close. It was awkward. After my husband prayed, the words that finally entered my mind and demanded to be spoken surprised me.

"You're healed." I said the words cautiously.

She opened her eyes and declared she could see clearly.

I skeptically asked, "Are you sure?" (Some great believer I turned out to be!) She confirmed that she could see across the room.

She returned to the DMV the next day and received her driver's license. That was nine years ago. She still has her driver's license today and reports that the "floaters" that used to obscure her vision have never returned. Even now as I relay this story, I'm in awe with an edge of disbelief.

It's a strange family story for us, in part because during the same season, we had committed to praying every day for my mom, who was struggling with neuropathy. She described the pain as "walking on needles." She stayed with us several days a week and watched our daughters while my husband and I worked. She was like a second mother to my girls. We loved her, and she took good care of us. The remarkable thing I always noticed about my mom was her deep well of patience. Pain never diminished this for her. She was never short tempered with her granddaughters. She even moved energetically for their sake, although I know it cost her a lot. We prayed fervently for her to have relief from the chronic pain in her feet, but relief never came for her. In fact, two years later she developed ALS, a completely unrelated condition, and died six months after the diagnosis.

Why one person is healed through prayer and another is not is a question that has been asked through the ages. It seems how God reveals himself to humanity will remain a mystery. I suspect that if it was a predictable pattern it wouldn't be much of a relationship. It might tempt us to manipulate the formula in our favor, reducing our relationship with God to a simple exchange of commodities. Maybe that's why big "M" miracles seem to be the exception and not the norm.

How this book came to be

I'd like to share with you the latest little "m" miracle in my life, but let me first give you some context. Last year, I was diagnosed with B Cell Lymphoma. Once the twelve-centimeter mass in my chest was identified, I knew I wasn't going to die, but it would be a difficult six months. My course of treatment meant a hospital stay every three weeks, during which I received ninety-two straight hours of chemo.

My biggest fear, of course, was my children and the impact this trauma might have on them. My next fear was whether I would be able to continue working and support my family. My husband and I are from Seattle. As Gen Xers, we've been caught in the insane cost of living increase brought-to the area by the tech industry. Finances are difficult. For many reasons, moving isn't a great option for us. It's stressful, but we manage. Well, we manage with both of our incomes. As someone who's self-employed, I was facing a scary possibility.

And yet, we made it through. With the amazing support of family and friends who propped me up, I was able to continue working. Good things came from the situation. My daughters had the chance to witness the best of humanity. Incredible love and support flowed from everyone we knew through cards, meals, rides, prayers, care packages, and just plain showing up and being present with us. My favorite memory of presence took place around my hospital bed, with my daughters and an older colleague of mine playing poker. This zesty gal had taught herself poker at the age of sixty, and she was just beginning to play professionally. What an amazing feat! Having her teach my daughters the game while sitting on my hospital bed, using Dove chocolates as poker chips, was a precious moment in time.

When I finished with chemo, I was ready to ride off into the sunset, but that's not how life unfolded. Three weeks after treatment I had a bad fall and dislocated my elbow. The orthopedic doctor explained that, for a dislocation to occur, the bones have to rip through the surrounding tissue. Yep! That sounds about right. When I fell, all I could do was moan on the ground, my cap askew on my bald head. A jogging couple came across me. While the husband called 911, the wife tried to comfort me. She noticed my bald head and said, "Oh, you're so brave."

I think I swore. I'm sad I did that. She was trying to be kind. But I'm not brave. I never signed up for cancer. It just happened to me, and I had to get through it. Plus, I was in horrific pain, and I just knew this was going to be a long recovery on top of an already difficult health year.

That turned out to be the case. Healing required an enormous amount of physical therapy to regain mobility in my arm. Then three months later, I developed a secondary condition that's incredibly painful called frozen shoulder. I couldn't catch a break. I have many good days and find creative ways to manage with limited mobility, but I also have some discouraging days. This is where I recently learned about little "m" miracles.

A couple of months ago, a dark cloud of discouragement hung over my head. The fear was the same as it was last year during cancer treatment: Will I be able to keep working? Will chronic pain force me to stop with my therapy practice? This thought devastated me. As a daughter of parents who lost their house to foreclosure, poverty often feels just a few steps away. Sadly, my father never recovered mentally after losing his ability to provide for his family. He disappeared and became estranged from us. I'm well aware that fear plays tricks on us. In its attempt to warn us of danger ahead, anxiety paints a nasty picture of the future.

On this particular day, I was under anxiety's grip as I struggled with grueling pain. I reached out to my prayer group—four women who have been my companions for two decades now. I shared my discouragement with them. They held that pain with me, and then they did what they do best: They prayed! Of course, I was hoping for a big rescue from God, either in the form of complete healing from pain or a monetary windfall to pay medical bills. But, that didn't happen. Instead God began to surprise me with little "m" miracles. My discouraging thoughts shifted from "Can I keep going after all I've been through?" to "Wow! Look at you! You're making it through this." The change in thought was enough to lift the smothering cloud of discouragement.

Although I believe big "M" miracles exist, I began to wonder how much of that belief was interfering in my relationship with God? Could discovering the little "m's" help me find peace regardless of how the prayer chips fell? Stockpiled disappointments had kept me circling the same conversational pleas with God. I was growing weary of the conversation and even avoiding it altogether.

I decided it was time to observe my surroundings and notice the little "m" miracles that appear every day. With Lent approaching, I chose to make awareness my chief Lenten practice. On each of the forty days, I'd investigate something in the natural world and, during my daily walks, I'd meditate on that aspect of creation. So, I took forty Lenten days to do just that.

What I received in return was an incredible gift of perspective: seeing myself in the context of physical space and history. By stepping away from seeing myself as the center of the Universe, I was strangely comforted. But what I found to be even more important is that it opened me up to new and life-affirming conversations with God. I may be a speck in time and history, but I'm a speck in a relationship with the One who created it all.

Themes

Through this forty-day meditation, three important themes emerged for me: 1) the relationship community within the Godhead, 2) the recycling nature of God, and 3) the relational nature of all things. These themes presented themselves over and over again through the varying meditations.

The first surprising theme was the relationship within God—God, Christ, and the Holy Spirit and their response to the unfolding of creation. Every artist knows the thrill of watching a creative vision come to life. Can you imagine the reaction within God, as they together, spoke light, and witnessed the first day separated from night? We know that creation isn't just some cosmic energy flowing into place; the development of our world took thought and execution. Our understanding of this is, in part, shaped because we know God rested on the seventh day. In order to rest, there had to be work. Imagining that relationship within God, and the fulfillment of this creative outpouring they enjoyed together, stimulated in me a sense of honor to be invited into this world, into their shared vision.

The second theme wasn't wholly surprising but delightful to recognize, and that's the nature of God as a recycler. Whether it comes to water, air, or rock, these systems replenish themselves. This continual living environment has flowed through the ages. Again, it's an honor to be invited to live in such a diverse and sustainable ecosystem. I found myself incredibly grateful for the many layered details in creation that drive this continual flow of life, whether it's the breaking down of rocks into soil that makes its rich chemicals accessible to plants or the water system moving from glaciers to clouds that ensures we have clean water.

The third theme also wasn't surprising considering the nature of God. Every part of creation is relational. No part exists without a relationship to other aspects of creation. There was, however, one very surprising realization. One species is seemingly not necessary to sustain this ever-recycling life on Earth: humans! This is as unsettling as it is mystifying. Plants are essential for oxygen, which means soil is necessary, thereby making rocks a foundational part of this delicate system. Plant life, of course, is only possible due to the water system that's supported by the atmosphere. Birds move seeds and help with pollination. Other animals perpetuate the ecosystem along in varying ways. Even dung beetles are more essential than humans in keeping this planet going. And yet, we've been invited to this blue marble of a planet that's teeming with a richly diverse life force. What shall we do with this invitation?

We have been invited, and it's an important question for us to consider. What is our response to this incredible gift called Earth? What is our response to the One who made it all and formed us from dust and breathed life into our being?

How To Use This Book

This devotional was originally created through the season of Lent, but it can be used any time of the year. Lent is an ancient practice of fasting leading up to Easter. Church seasons are meant to develop different disciplines in our faith; for example, Advent is the season for expectant waiting. However, we recognize that these human rhythms occur throughout the year and not just in seasons. In fact, the old Catholic practice of eating fish on Fridays was meant to mimic Lent. The abstaining of beef or other rich meats on Friday was considered a fast leading up to Sunday, the day of rest and feasting, much like an Easter celebration. That was a weekly rhythm for many centuries in the church, representing discipline paired with celebration. And so, too, this devotional—with or without fasting—can be used in any season.

Lent

Welcome to the desert as we companion Jesus for forty days. Lent is the six-week period leading up to Easter beginning with Ash Wednesday. Often this season is accompanied with a practice that involves giving up something for the forty days of Lent (i.e., fasting). The Lenten season mirrors that period of time when Jesus entered the desert for forty days after his baptism and before he entered into his ministry. Jesus fasted while in the desert. That was an especially necessary time for Jesus to turn his attention toward God and further develop that attunement—not only to resist the temptation he encountered in the desert, but also in preparation for the ministry he was about to enter. For us, fasting provides a tangible reminder throughout our day to turn our attention toward Jesus. As we notice the missing item, we're prompted to redirect our thoughts.

My family often practices some type of fasting during Lent and, for a while now, my children have included add-ons as well. For example, one year my youngest daughter decided to read a Psalm a day.

With this year's Lent, I chose to fast from sugar along with adding something new to my routine: a new mindset during my morning walks. I meditated on the depth and breadth of God's creation during these walks. Then throughout the day, whenever I craved sugar, I redirected my thoughts to that aspect in nature that I was intentionally meditating on, allowing that to be my entry into conversation with God.

A Daily Rhythm

Through the years I have learned that God is a boundary keeper. God will not encroach where we have not given invitation. This is respectful of God, but it sometimes takes us a long time to ask for that living water to enter an area of our life that is parched. That's why a discipline such as this Lent devotional is helpful for hacking away the weeds and thorns in our soul to expose those areas. This happens when each day, in some small way, we make the effort to show up and recognize the One who is greater than us.

You can do this simply by not fighting against your nature. Try closing your eyes and taking a few deep breaths. Then ground yourself to this present moment by opening your eyes and noticing a few details in your environment. Then do a full body scan from the top of your head to the tips of your toes, noticing the internal workings of your body. If you're relaxed, practice gratefulness and thank God for that relaxed state. If you notice tension in your body, without self-judgment, welcome that tension and simply invite God into that space. Continue breathing and thank God that tension and emotions are ways that our body gives us feedback in order to navigate the world, much like a pilot with a panel of instruments. Ask God to tune up your radar system so it will be a helpful resource for you as you enter this journey for the next forty days.

Each day, set some time aside for this devotional. This can be done first thing in the morning or possibly during a daily walk. Choose when in your day you want to be mindful of creation. You can even begin the devotion by grounding yourself in the present moment with the breathing exercise. Then read the daily devotion. Use the description and the picture to begin your observation of that devotional topic. During this time, take a few moments to envision this part of creation—its color, texture, and how the system works and interplays with other aspects of the natural world.

After thinking about this item more concretely, here are three considerations: 1) think about this item from God's perspective and what it was like to see its development unfolding; 2) spend time thanking God for this aspect of creation, considering the gift it is in your life; or 3) allow this part of creation to become a metaphor for your own life, revealing an area in your life that needs attention, and simply invite God into that space.

At the end of each devotion are suggested scripture readings for further study. You can look up the verses in your Bible or you can find them in the back of this book..

The Present Moment

Allow these items to spark your curiosity as you enter a conversation with God. In addition to developing your conversation with God, notice that the natural world often brings us into the present moment. When we use one of our five senses to enter the present moment, our nervous system relaxes. It's here that we often discover we are safe. It's when our thoughts periscope through time that we generally experience stress, either leaning toward depression (thoughts dwelling on the past) or anxiousness (thoughts projecting into the future). Enjoy coming into this present moment, noticing your surroundings, and being in the company of the great *I Am*. This is the name God gave when Moses asked, "Who are you?" You can't get more present moment than that!

Day 1: *Ash Wednesday*
Stars

There's between 100 and 400 billion stars in the Milky Way alone, and in the universe, there's an estimated 1,000, 000,000,000,000,000,000,000,000—more than a billion trillion stars! That's a staggering amount for the human mind to comprehend. Let's look at what it takes for an individual star to come into existence. A star is birthed inside a cold dark cloud of dust and hydrogen, where a quiet tug-of-war begins. The cloud itself wants to dissipate, like smoke in the air, but gravity pulls this cloud inward. This creates a balance between gas pressure pushing out and gravity pulling in. Gravity eventually wins, and the material in the center of the disc crunches down, becoming denser and compressed. This pressure causes heat and, at 18 million degrees, a miraculous transformation takes place. Hydrogen atoms fuse together to form helium and, with a burst of nuclear energy, the stars begin to shine. However, the stars are initially obscured by the surrounding dust and gas. Over the next few million years, winds blow this surrounding material into spectacular swirling patterns. Once the dust and gas are completely blown away, we're finally able to see this beautiful new place where a star has been born.

REFLECTIONS

Consider what a thrill that must have been for God, Christ, and the Holy Spirit to speak light and see the first stars hanging in the universe. Imagine the joy and their interactions together as the beginning of creation unfolded. What happens to you when you consider that the One who spoke stars into being is currently present with you, right here, right now?

Suggested scripture reading for further study: Psalm 147:4-5, Psalm 19:1, Zephaniah 3:17 (ESV)

Day 2:

Particles

Elementary particles are the smallest known building blocks of the universe. They have no internal structure, which means they have zero-dimensional points that take up no space. This is the foundational fabric of all matter. Everything we can see and touch is made of matter. It is all the stuff of the universe. Things that are not made of matter include energy and ideas like peace and love. Particles are so small that you would have to put about 100,000 particles in a line to equal the width of a human hair! Matter exists in three states: solid, liquid, or gas. In each of these states, particles are arranged and move differently. Solids contain particles that are tightly packed whereas liquids contain particles that are more loosely packed; in gases, the particles are even more spread apart. Matter can change from one state to another. When solids change to liquids, the particles become more loosely packed in relation to one another. A melting ice cube is a good example of a solid transforming into liquid. When liquids change to gases, the particles become even more loosely packed. We see this when steam rises from boiling water. For this change, it takes energy to move matter from one state to another. Heat must be applied to change solid to liquid and liquid to gas. The opposite is also true. To change liquid into a solid, energy must be removed. When particles become cold, they move together and form a solid, like ice. Even though they're minute, particles form all that we see and touch.

REFLECTIONS

What happens when you think about the smallest foundational building blocks of our universe, the tiny particles found across history and space? How might this fabric have first appeared to God in the beginning moments of creation compared to now after the unfolding of time? What is your response when you consider this fabric that holds us all together?

Suggested scripture reading for further study: Psalm 111:2, Psalm 90:1-2, and Revelation 1:8

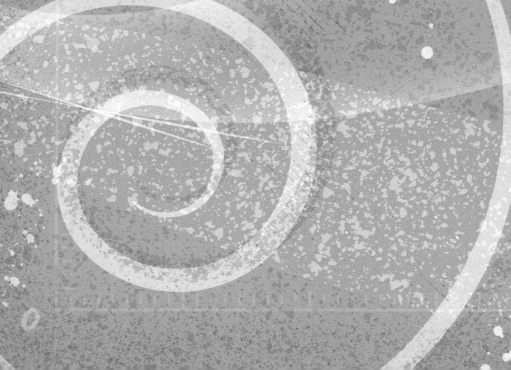

Day 3:
Smiles

British researchers recently discovered that one smile stimulates the pleasure center of the brain in the same way as receiving $25,000 in cash! Astonishingly, children smile an estimated four hundred times a day whereas adults only smile around twenty times a day. This may explain the joy we often experience around children, especially when we consider the communal nature of smiling. It's nearly impossible to frown when we look at another person who is smiling. Our instinct is to mimic the smile, and we do that, in part, to discern the type of smile we're seeing. Is it a synthetic or real one? A real smile involves the zygomatic major (raising the corners of the mouth) and the orbicularis oculi (raising the cheeks and producing crow's feet around the eyes). In research performed at the University of Clermont-Ferrand, people were asked to discern smiling faces; they then repeated the exercise with a pencil in their mouths. When their own ability to smile was impaired, so was their ability to discern a real versus synthetic smile. Our instinct to discern provides us with a gift as it causes us to automatically smile when we see others smiling. Not only does smiling make us feel better, but we also share that experience when we smile at others.

REFLECTIONS

In your mind's eye, imagine God smiling at you. What is your response to the genuine joy in God's eyes? Consider why it was important to God to create smiles? What is one simple way, like a smile, that you can spread joy to someone else today?

Suggested scripture reading for further study: Numbers 6:24-26 and Proverbs 17:22

Day 4:
Cherry Blossoms

These five-petal delicate flowers actually begin developing the summer prior to their full bloom the following spring. A hormone released in the leaves stops their growth at the end of summer. Cherry trees use two mechanisms to recognize seasonal change: daylight hours and temperature. A decrease in sunlight signals to the tree to start its dormancy phase. This rest phase is necessary for producing blooms and, later, fruit. Cherry trees need 800 to 1,200 chilling hours, where temperatures are below 45°F. After several warm days in a row, the blooms are triggered to begin developing once again. Once in full bloom, these beautiful flowers only last one week. Their short time span is part of the gift for us. The fleeting nature draws people out to enjoy their splendor. Of course, the tree doesn't show off for our sake. It's about reproduction. A plant or tree that depends on wind for pollination generally has fewer flowers and often the flowers are duller in color. The more fragrant and brighter the flower, the more bees and birds are drawn to their petals to initiate pollination. The cherry tree is a stunner for nature's pollinators.

REFLECTIONS

Cherry blossoms need rest before continuing their growth. This rhythm of rest and work seems to repeat itself on many different levels in creation. This sacred dance must be important to God. What fruit blooms when you follow this rhythm of rest and work? Beyond the weekly rhythm of rest and work, consider how you respond to seasons of dormancy? How is God possibly at work in those hidden spaces during those seasons?

Suggested scripture reading for further study: Genesis 2:2, Matthew 11:28-30, and Philippians 1:6

Day 5:

First Sunday in Lent

Pause from the devotion & read *Genesis 1*

In the beginning God created the heavens and the earth. Now the earth was formless and empty, darkness was over the surface of the deep, and the Spirit of God was hovering over the waters. And God said, "Let there be light," and there was light.

God saw that the light was good, and he separated the light from the darkness. God called the light "day," and the darkness he called "night." And there was evening, and there was morning—the first day.

Day 6:
Honey Bees

Honey bees use an intelligent communication pattern to instruct their fellow workers on where to find the best food source. It's called the waggle dance. After finding a new source of nectar, the honey bee returns to the nest and vibrates her belly in order to gain the attention of her sisters. Once she has their attention, she proceeds to dance in a figure eight. The waggle portion of the dance points to the exact angle to the sun and distance from the hive of the source. This complex navigational system means that bees have an internal clock. Even after several hours in the dark hive, they know the exact location of the sun. They can even calibrate to latitude and length of day. Gravity within the hive helps with communication. If the bee waggles directly upward, that means fly toward the sun; if the bee waggles downward, it means fly away from the sun. A three o'clock waggle means fly ninety degrees to the sun. Her communication can accurately pinpoint a nectar source up to six kilometers away. The length of the waggle communicates distance. Every second marks one kilometer. During a short season, the colonists visit up to 1.5 million flowers and make around ninety kilograms of honey.

REFLECTIONS

If God equips bees with this kind of internal clock and compass, what types of internal gifts has God given to you? How does your tendency toward distraction possibly cut you off from these gifts? How might you stay in the present, attuned to all that God has for you in this expansive moment?

Suggested scripture reading for further study: 1 Corinthians 12:4-6, Isaiah 30:21, and Proverbs 24:14

Day 7:
Tectonic Plates

Tectonic plates make up the Earth's outer shell. Churning currents in the molten rocks below propel the plates like a conveyor belt in disrepair. The places where these plates meet or divide create the Earth's most interesting geological formations. This is a long game. The plates move at a rate of one to two inches a year. Convergent plates, where these landmasses smash into each other, cause the crust to crumple and buckle, giving rise to mountain ranges. Mt. Everest, the highest point on Earth, may be a little bit taller tomorrow than today. Divergent boundaries occur at the mid ocean ridges. Here, fresh lava reaches the surface, creating undersea mountains or volcanos that sometimes reach the surface, like the creation of Iceland. Where tectonic plates slip horizontally past one another, the Earth's crust is neither created nor destroyed. The grinding action between the plates at a transform boundary results in earthquakes. There's now .evidence that the recycling nature of the Earth's crust, caused by the shifting plates, is what leads to a stabilized atmosphere. The creation of coastlines, the movement of tides, along with slabs of rock diving under each other, provide our oceans with the necessary chemistry to support life. The Earth is definitely in a constant state of change. Our planet looks very different than it did 250 million years ago, when there was only one continent and one ocean.

REFLECTIONS

Change is ever present in creation. Even the foundational crust of the Earth shifts and moves. How do you accept change in your life? Do you surrender your vulnerabilities to God when the tectonic plates in your life collide, divide, or grind past each other? When have you feared a change leading up to it and then looked back and seen God's hand at work?

Suggested scripture reading for further study Psalm 46:1-3, Psalm 73:26, and Hebrews 13:8

Day 8: Plankton

Water makes up three quarters of our Earth. In these vast bodies of water are tiny living organisms called plankton. They are so small that even the width of a human hair outdoes them in size. That's tiny! But they are abundant. They may seem like aimless drifters, but they play a vital role on Earth. Not only does the marine ecosystem depend on plankton as a food source, but plankton is also responsible for fifty percent of all photosynthesis and ninety-five percent of recycled organic matter. Through the process of photosynthesis, plankton absorbs carbon dioxide and eventually drifts to the ocean floor, creating what has become our oil and gas reserves. Without plankton, there would be no fuel. But we have an even bigger dependency on this minuscule creature. Plankton, like all other vegetation, uses solar energy to convert carbon dioxide into carbohydrates. As the Earth's largest plant source, plankton is responsible for giving us at least fifty percent of the oxygen we need to breathe.

REFLECTIONS

The triune God went to great lengths and detail to ensure that you have sustainable life. What would your life look like if you noticed these extraordinary gifts every day? As you pause and notice your breath in this moment, pay close attention to how it feels to have air fill your lungs. Spend some time thanking God for plankton.

Suggested scripture reading for further study: Psalm 104:24-25, Philippians 4:19, and Psalm 150:6

Day 9: Bag Bugs

Bag bugs are a member of the moth family. During their cocoon phase, they build the craziest looking houses for themselves on their backs. I saw a picture of a bag bug with what looked like a tiny Lincoln Log cabin on its back. They use whatever they can find in their environment, including leaves, twigs, and even feathers. These are effective camouflage as you can barely see the tip of the worm-like bug peeking its head out. The cases of the bagworm moth are incredibly tough and very difficult to break open. As their cases are composed of materials from their habitat, they are naturally camouflaged from predators, such as birds and other insects. The structure is strongly bonded to the bug and takes a great deal of force to be removed given the relative size and weight of the actual structure. There are 1,300 species of bag bugs, and they can be found worldwide.

REFLECTIONS

The bag bug recognizes that, in order to do the hard work of transformation, we need to feel safe and protected. What protective covering does God give you? What does the architecture of your boundaries look like? The Psalms describe our relationship with God as dwelling in God's house. How does dwelling in this Most High place possibly contribute to this covering?

Suggested scripture reading for further study: Psalm 3:3, Psalm 62:7-8, and Psalm 27:4-5

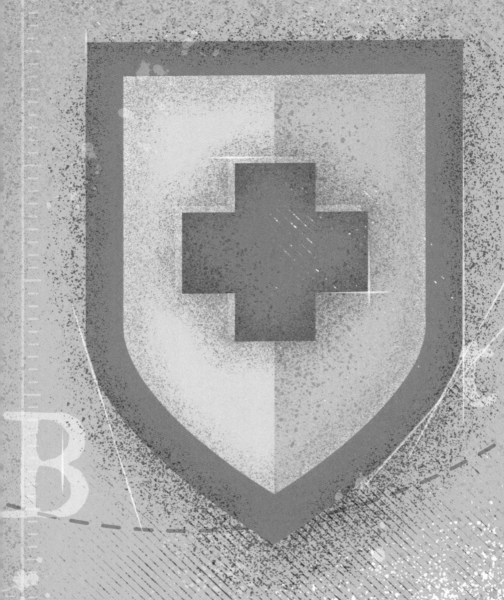

Day 10:
Immune System

Our body is naturally primed to heal itself through our complex immune system, which functions like an army. We have a series of cells ready for battle to guard against bacteria and viruses. Each layer of defense is quickly supported by several other systems. Our immune system has twelve different jobs, ranging from communicating to activating other cells, producing antibodies, killing enemies, engaging in strategic decision-making, and even remembering enemies for the next battle. When the first barrier of the immune system, our skin, is breached and bacteria have entered, huge guard cells approach the scene. Messenger proteins quickly communicate location and urgency. If these soldiers can't eradicate the invading force, dendritic cells are activated. These large warriors collect cells from the enemy, ripping them into pieces, which helps them discern the nature of the enemy. Dendritic cells make a critical decision: Does the situation call for anti-bacteria or virus killers? Once the decision is made, the communicators travel to lymph nodes in a day, where billions of T and B cells are awaiting to be activated. B cells produce antibodies that bind to antigens and neutralize them. T cells help get rid of good cells that have already been infected. Memory cells help reinforce this victory by remembering antigens that have already attacked the body. This is how we build up immunity.

REFLECTIONS

Helping a body move toward health seems important to God. What are ways you can come into alignment with God's system? What do you need to yield or do to encourage mental, physical, and spiritual health?

Suggested scripture reading for further study: Psalm 139:13-14, Psalm 147:3, and 1 Peter 5:10

Day 11:

Clouds

All clouds share the same basic ingredient: water. They're made up of water droplets or ice crystals. When billions of these droplets come together, they become a visible cloud. Although you can't see it, water is all around us. The air contains water even on the clearest summer day. The main source of evaporation comes from the surfaces of oceans and lakes, soil, and transpiration (the release of water by plants). As the sun warms the air, the molecules rise, condense, and gather together when they reach colder air. That's when the water in the air becomes visible. The water droplets eventually release back to Earth in the form of rain and snow, starting the water cycle all over again. There's a reason we tend to see more clouds on cold days. Hot air can hold more water vapor. In cooler weather, water vapors condense together, forming clouds. These formations are actually quite heavy. A single cloud weighs several hundred tons. They do not fall because warm air currents push against the tiny droplets, keeping them from crashing to the ground. Naturally, higher wispy clouds (cirrus) are made of ice crystals because of the colder temperature. When we see these white strands, it often means fair weather. Low-hanging clouds shaped like flat sheets (stratus) may produce a light drizzle. The white fluffy cotton-ball-like clouds (cumulus) rarely produce precipitation when they are scattered through the sky in separate piles.

REFLECTIONS

God provides us with a continual flow of water through this natural recycling system. How do you feel about this gift and the impact it has on your life? Do you notice this ever-present system overhead and the ability it often gives you to anticipate the weather?

Suggested scripture reading for further study: Psalm 104:2-4, Psalm 147:7-8, and John 4:14

Day 12:
Second Sunday in Lent

Pause from the devotion &
read *Psalm 139*

If I go up to the heavens, you are there;

if I make my bed in the depths, you are there.

If I rise on the wings of the dawn,

if I settle on the far side of the sea,

even there your hand will guide me,

your right hand will hold me fast.

Day 13:
Douglas Fir Trees

Douglas firs are the giants of trees. Coastal Douglas firs can reach 250 feet tall. Native Americans used these massive trees for medicinal purposes in treating stomachaches, headaches, rheumatism, and the common cold. Scientists are now discovering that trees are cooperators instead of competitors. British Columbia forester Suzanne Simard explained how Douglas fir trees share carbon with their neighboring dormant deciduous trees and will, in turn, ask for help when they are in need due to pests or disease. Trees communicate their needs and send each other nutrients via a network of latticed fungi buried in the soil. When Douglas fir trees are injured, a couple of things happen. The Douglas fir dumps its carbon into the network, and it's taken up by the ponderosa pine. Then the defense enzymes of the Douglas fir and the ponderosa pine are up-regulated in response to this injury. Those two responses—the carbon transfer and the defense signal—only happen where there's a mycorrhizal network intact. When scientists severed this network, the responses didn't occur. As we discover how trees speak to each other, it's becoming apparent that the forest isn't a bunch of individual species, but is instead a collective organism.

REFLECTIONS

Why is this communal system important to God? What happens when you see yourself as part of a collective organism rather than a competitor? How does this possibly shift your view of the people around you and even your surrounding environment?

Suggested scripture reading for further study: 1 Corinthians 12:25-27 and Galatians 6:2

Day 14:
Animal Heartbeats

An adult human's resting heart rate is normally 60 to 100 beats per minute. That's slow compared to the shrew, clocking in at over 1,000 beats per minute—or sixteen times a second. Heart rates generally correlate with animal size. Larger animals tend to have slower heart rates while smaller animals have faster heart rates. For example, the pygmy shrew, weighing less than an ounce, has the fastest heart rate at 1,200 beats per minute. Meanwhile, the 100-foot long blue whale, the biggest animal on Earth, weighing up to 330,000 pounds, with its heart weighing as much as 400 pounds, has the slowest heart rate. A study by Stanford University discovered that, when blue whales dive for food, their heart slows to as few as two beats per minute. Other animals have multiple hearts. Cephalopods like squid and octopus usually have three hearts: Two hearts pump blood to the gills while a third circulates it to the rest of the body. Yet some animals have no heart at all. Sea stars and other echinoderms do not have a heart, nor do they have blood to pump with one. Starfish have millions of tiny hair-like structures called cilia that beat constantly, pumping seawater via a system of internal pipes and bags. Their internal cavity also has all the various cells needed for transporting nutrients and immune cells.

REFLECTIONS

Does God have a heart? Just as blood is the life force in animals and humans, what is the life force in God? If love is God's life force, how are you a part of that force?

Suggested scripture reading for further study: Proverbs 4:23, 1 John 4:8, and John 15:16-17

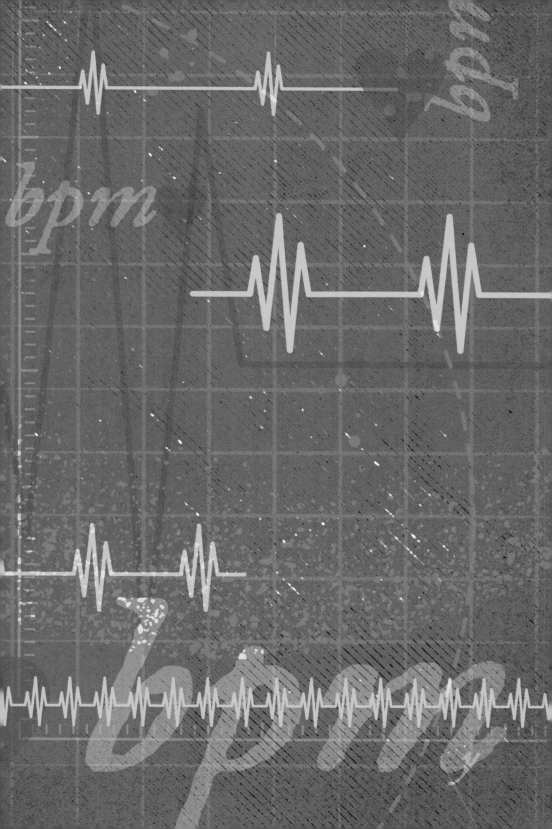

Day 15:
North/South Axis

A variety of species seem to detect the Earth's magnetic field, and some animals, such as migratory birds, rely on it for navigation. Just like a compass that points north, these internal systems discern the Earth's north/south axis. Interestingly, animals seem to align along this axis for other purposes, not just navigational reasons. Studies have shown that birds' preferred landing direction is along the north–south axis. Cows even sense the Earth's magnetic field and use it to line up their bodies so they face either north or south when grazing or resting. German researchers used satellite images from Google Earth to discover that herds were lining up in a north–south line, like a living compass needle. Of course, this navigational system is especially helpful when traveling long distances. During their long 8,000-mile migrations around the Atlantic Ocean, young loggerhead sea turtles can not only detect the field's intensity, but also its inclination, the angle at which magnetic field lines intersect the Earth. Turtles use these two pieces of information as navigational markers. The most bizarre discovery related to this internal system is that dogs use the Earth's magnetic field to align their bowel and bladder movements. According to a Czech Republic study, dogs prefer to relieve themselves along a north–south axis and they will actively avoid going to the bathroom in an east-west direction.

REFLECTIONS

Sensitivity to a force that is unseen is a type of navigational tool. What helps you pay attention to the Spirit's inner leading in your life? Is there any Inner Guidance right now that you're not acknowledging? How can you take steps to investigate and honor this navigational tool?

Suggested scripture reading for further study: John 14:25-26 and Romans 8:26-27

Day 16:
Size *of the* Universe

The sun is 93 million miles away, which—because of the speed of light—means we're seeing what it looked like 8.3 minutes ago. The next closest star is 4.3 light years away, so we're actually seeing the light that radiated from it 4.3 years ago. All other stars are even farther, thousands of light years away. A light year is 5.8 trillion miles. Scientists estimate that the Milky Way is 150,000 light years across and the observable Universe is about 93 billion light years in diameter. For some perspective, take a minuscule object, like a grain of sand, and hold it at arm's length. The sand grain covers just a tiny patch of sky. When the Hubble Space Telescope did just that and observed a tiny patch of dark sky for a total of fifty-five hours, it found more than 10,000 galaxies. If this picture is typical, scientists concluded there must be about 100 billion galaxies in the observable cosmos. Each galaxy would have about 100 billion stars on average, and stars typically have roughly ten planets and hundreds or thousands of asteroids and comets. Since this initial study, new research has discovered faint galaxies that can be particularly difficult to observe. With this new information, astrophysicist Brian Koberlein explained, "Rather than a Universe filled with 100 billion galaxies, there are likely 2 trillion galaxies in the observable Universe. That's about 200 galaxies for every man, woman and child on Earth." This alone is a staggering thought, but remember that the Universe is continually expanding.

REFLECTIONS

The sheer number of galaxies in the Universe indicates that variety and diversity seem important to God. Often there isn't one type of species, but several variations of that species. There's not just one galaxy, but rather 2 trillion. It seems God's creative power is vast and varied. What happens when you consider the size and diversity of God's creation?

Suggested scripture reading for further study: Psalm 147:4-5, Psalm 103:11-12, and Acts 17:24-28

10^{12}

|———————————————————————|

y

Day 17: Mathematics

There are thousands of languages in the world today, but math is the only true universal language. Math is a universal language because the principles and foundations of math are the same everywhere around the world. Ten plus ten equals twenty whether you write it using Arabic numerals (10 + 10 = 20) or Roman numerals (X + X = XX). The concept of twenty items is the same no matter where you are in the world. Italian astronomer and physicist Galileo stated, "Mathematics is the language in which God has written the universe. [The universe] cannot be read until we have learnt the language and become familiar with the characters in which it is written. It is written in mathematical language, and the letters are triangles, circles and other geometrical figures, without which means it is humanly impossible to comprehend a single word." Mathematical symbols, as well as their meanings, syntax, and grammar, are the same throughout the world. According to the mathematician Anne Marie Helminstine, "A mathematical equation may be stated in words to form a sentence that has a noun and a verb, just like a sentence in a spoken language. For example: 3 + 5 = 8 could be stated as 'Three added to five equals eight'."

REFLECTIONS

What is the language used by the triune God? It seems that math, in part, has to be their language. We often don't attribute warmth or life to math, but is it possible that God views math as a foundational force? How has math guided humanity, like a treasure map, to breathtaking discoveries on the micro and macro levels?

Suggested scripture reading for further study: Colossians 1:17 and Luke 6:46-48

Day 18: Sunflowers

Each sunflower is actually thousands of tiny flowers. This is the seedbed for 1,000 to 2,000 seeds. Sunflowers generally grow five to six feet tall, although the tallest on record is thirty feet. The French word for sunflower is tournesol, which means "turns with the sun." A sunflower anticipates daybreak, much like a rooster does before starting to crow. At sunrise, sunflowers face east to greet the first rays, and they continue to move with the sun until it sets in the west. Overnight, the sunflower head swings back around so it faces east at dawn. This internal clock seems to adjust even as dawn changes by three minutes each day. By following the sun all day, the sunflower grows faster and puts on more biomass. This seems possible with sunlight as the cue. Genes that control growth on the east side of the stem are more active during the day whereas genes on the west side are more active overnight. Scientists suspect that the sunflower's leaves somehow contribute to this tracking system as the rhythmic movement stops when mature leaves are cut off. The movement gradually reduces as the plant approaches flowering. Mature sunflowers stay facing east. The warmth gathered in the east-facing sunflower attracts more pollinators.

REFLECTIONS

How can you orient yourself toward the light of God throughout the day? What little and big rays of light are in your life that you can thank God for? There are always shadows in life, but how can you focus on the light and cultivate gratefulness?

Suggested scripture reading for further study: Psalm 96:12-13a, Philippians 4:8, and Psalm 119:105

Day 19:
Third Sunday in Lent

Pause from the devotion &
read *Psalm 96*

Let the heavens rejoice, let the earth be glad;

let the sea resound, and all that is in it.

Let the fields be jubilant, and everything in them;

let all the trees of the forest sing for joy.

Let all creation rejoice before the LORD,

Day 20: Moon

The Earth's moon is unique in our solar system and may be rare in the entire universe. Astronomers from the University of Zurich created models of the early solar system to show why planet-stabilizing moons are rare. "Small moons would easily form, with an immediate effect on the planet's spin. But some could spiral into the planet, while others could quickly leave the orbit." Thankfully our moon is safely in place, making our home more livable by moderating the Earth's wobble. Without it, astronomers have predicted that the Earth's tilt could vary by as much as eighty-five degrees and eventually place the sun above the poles rather than directly above the equator. Our moon orbits the Earth once every 27.322 days, and it takes approximately twenty-seven days for it to rotate once on its axis. As a result, the Moon appears to be almost perfectly still. Scientists call this synchronous rotation. The rotations of the Earth and Moon are so in sync we only see one side of the Moon all the time. The Earth and Moon are also tidally locked, which contributes to our stable climate. The Moon's gravitational pull generates something called the tidal force, which causes the Earth—and its water—to bulge out on the side closest to the Moon and the side farthest from the Moon. These bulges of water are high tides, which happen twice a day. Tidal currents affect the weather by stirring the ocean waters, mixing arctic water with warmer tropic water. The Moon itself has no atmosphere and only about one-sixth of the Earth's gravity.

REFLECTIONS

The ebb and flow of tides have created a rhythm for many human civilizations—not to mention the Moon's orbit around the Earth and its impact on how we organize our calendars. What rhythms in your life keep you in sync with God?

Suggested scripture reading for further study: Genesis 1:14-19, Psalm 104:19, and Matthew 11:28-30 (MSG)

Day 21: Magnetic Field

Life on Earth developed and continues to be sustained under the Earth's magnetic field, otherwise known as the magnetosphere shield. This shield sets us apart from other planets. The magnetosphere serves to deflect most of the solar wind from the sun. These charged particles would otherwise strip the ozone layer that protects the Earth from harmful ultraviolet radiation. Within the Earth's outer liquid core, convective kinetic energy is converted into electrical and magnetic energy, much like an electrical generator. This energy, along with the Earth's rotation on its axis, causes enough agitation that a magnetic field forms around the planet, radiating out from the Earth. On the side of the planet facing the sun, this shield is compressed due to the sheer force of arriving particles. Although most of these potentially harmful rays are deflected, the few particles that reach the night side can become trapped at the poles, allowing us to see the solar storm known as the aurora borealis in the northern hemisphere or aurora australis in the southern hemisphere. Thankfully, these storms, while visible, are still so high in the atmosphere that they don't pose any threat to the Earth.

REFLECTIONS

How did this perfectly balanced system that we call life on Earth occur to God? What propelled this outpouring of creation? Take time to express your appreciation to God for this amazing bio-diverse ecosystem guarded by an invisible but powerful protective shield. Consider the ways God provides you with a shield of protection in your life.

Suggested scripture reading for further study: Psalm 104:5, Psalm 3:3-4 (MSG), and Proverbs 30:5

Day 22: Hippos

Hippos are the third largest living land mammals, after elephants and white rhinos. They're the life force of African rivers. Known as the river horse, hippos spend up to sixteen hours a day in the water, cooling their bodies. Their eyes and nostrils are on the top of their head, which allows them to submerge most of their body and still breathe. Surprisingly, these water-loving animals can't swim. Their heavy bodies sink to the bottom, and they glide under water by pushing off of objects. Hippos secrete an interesting gel that protects their sensitive skin from sunburn. To further help protect their skin, they don't usually come out of the river to graze on grass until night. They can eat up to 100 pounds of grass in one meal. By daybreak, having eaten their fill, they return to their daytime resting area to digest and eventually eliminate. This natural process results in millions of tons of hippo dung entering Africa's aquatic ecosystems every year. As distasteful as that might seem, the hippos' deposits actually serve an important ecological function. Fish and other aquatic life feed on hippo dung. But even more importantly, the silicon from the grass supports single-celled organisms called diatoms, which are a type of plankton called phytoplankton. Ah, we're back to plankton!

REFLECTIONS

Thank God for plankton! Consider the balance of each ecosystem on Earth—the animals, plants, and atmospheric pressures that perpetuate life in each of these areas. We may not be a vital part of the Earth's ecosystem, but we are a part of the spiritual and emotional ecosystem in our communities. How can you, like the hippo, be who God created you to be and, in doing so, add to this spiritual/emotional ecosystem?

Suggested scripture reading for further study: Psalm 104:10-14, Romans 12:4-5, and Colossians 3:14-16

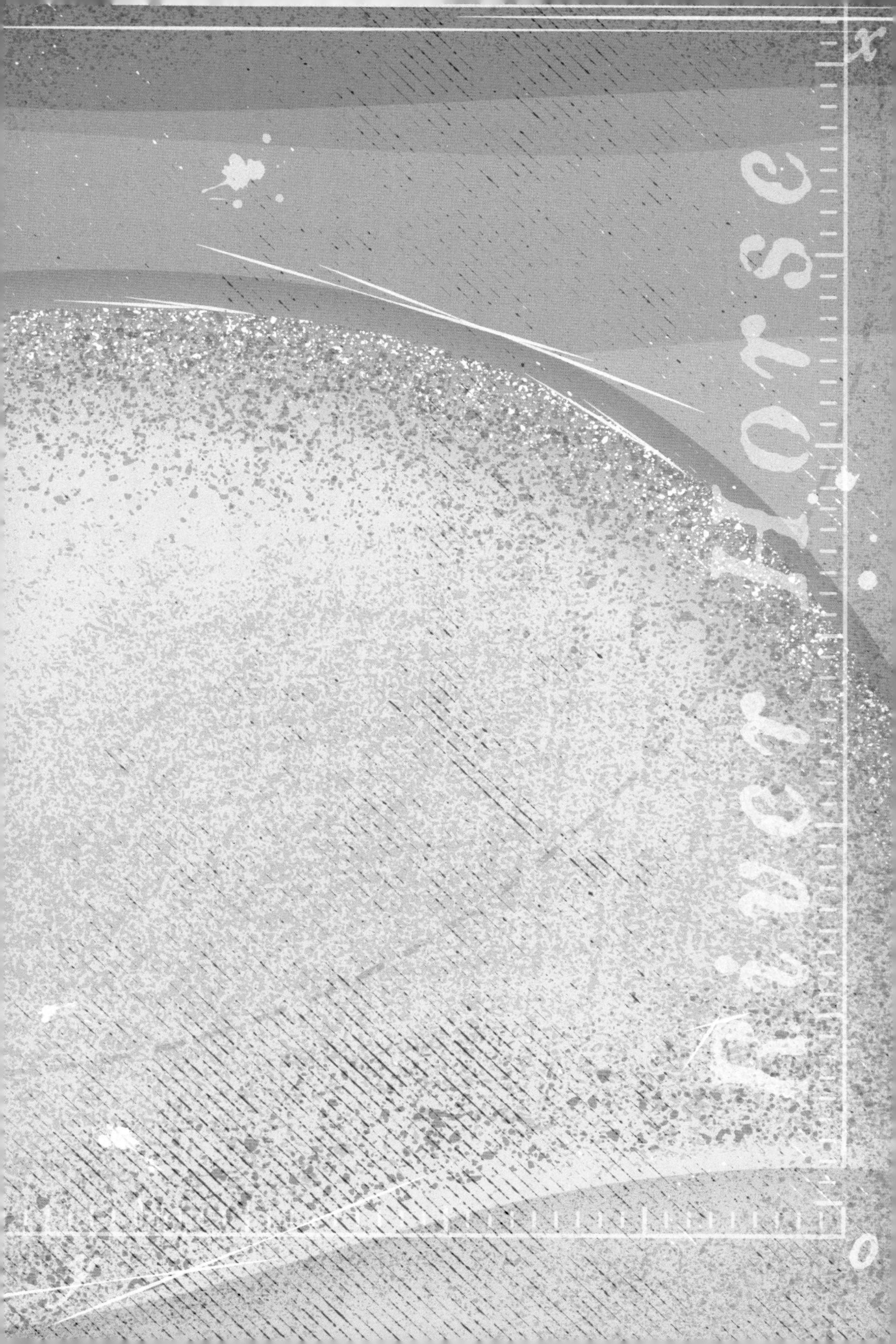
Universe

Day 23:

Light

Light is made up of little packets of energy called photons. These particles have zero mass and can't be split. Photons are produced when the atoms in an object heat up. Heat excites the electrons inside the atoms, and they gain extra energy. Light does not need matter to carry its wave-like energy. This means that light can travel through a vacuum—a completely airless space; sound, on the other hand, must travel through a solid, a liquid, or a gas. Nothing travels faster than light energy. It speeds through the vacuum of space at 186,400 miles per second. When light travels between two places (from the sun to the Earth or from a flashlight to a sidewalk), energy makes a journey. This energy travels in the form of waves—a vibrating pattern of electricity and magnetism that we call electromagnetic energy. Physicist Cathal O'Connel provided an eloquent description of light: "Light is an electric field tied up with a magnetic field, flying through space. You can think of the two fields as dance partners, wrapped up in an eternal embrace. To keep self-generating, both electric and magnetic components need to stay in step." These dance partners travel indefinitely until colliding with matter, when light is partly reflected and partly absorbed. Light is made of all of the colors of the rainbow. The everyday objects around us are actually white, colored, or black as well as opaque or transparent, depending on how the electrons in their atoms or molecules respond to the driving force of electromagnetic radiation. Objects appear to be different colors because they absorb some colors and reflect or transmit other colors. For example, a red apple absorbs all the colors of the rainbow except for red, causing the red light to reflect off the apple.

REFLECTIONS

Considering that light is dynamic energy and color, where in your life do you experience light? Are there places in your life today that could use more light? Are you willing to invite God's loving care and attention into those areas?

Suggested scripture reading for further study: Psalm 139:11-12, John 8:12, and 1 John 1:5-9 (MSG)

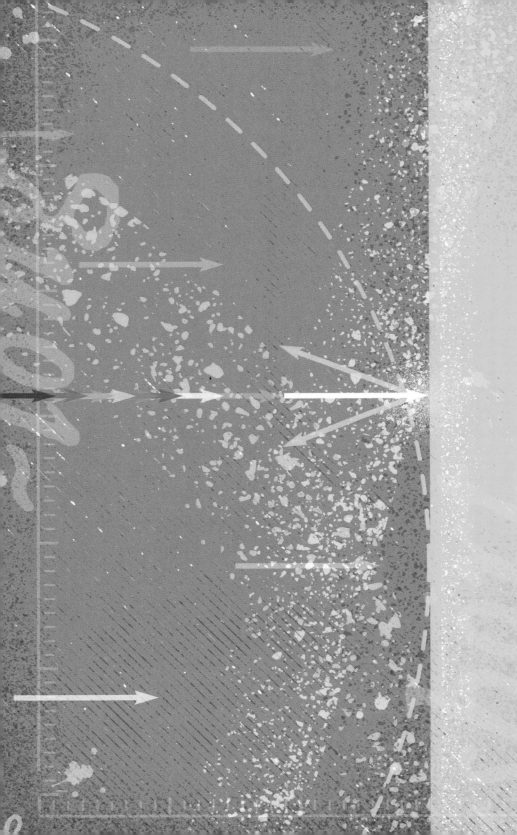

Day 24:
Leaves

Leaves are food-making machines for plants. A leaf is a flat, thin plant organ that uses the sun to make its own food, much like a solar panel. An important function of the leaf is photosynthesis, where light energy is turned into chemical energy. First, leaves use a chemical called chlorophyll to trap energy from the sun. The energy is then used to combine water from the soil and carbon dioxide gas from the air to make sugar for the plant. Lastly, oxygen is released during this process through pores in the back of the leaf. There are three layers to a leaf: the outer waxy epidermis, the spongy mesophyll, and the interior veins. The mesophyll is composed of chlorophyll-containing chloroplasts, which absorb sunlight and use the radiant energy in decomposing water into its elements (i.e., hydrogen and oxygen). The hydrogen obtained from water is combined with carbon dioxide to form the sugars that are transported through the veins as food energy to the plant. The oxygen released from green leaves replaces the oxygen removed from the atmosphere by plant and animal respiration. Leaves demonstrate recycling well by absorbing carbon in the atmosphere, transforming it into food for the plant, and releasing oxygen into the environment.

REFLECTIONS

How does this process make you think about the order of creation? What elements were in place before human and animal life were possible? How do you fit in this order?

Day 25:
Frontal Lobe *of*
the Human Brain

The frontal lobes are considered our emotional control center and home to our personality. Specifically, the frontal lobes are involved in motor function, problem solving, spontaneity, memory, language, initiation, judgment, impulse control, and social and sexual behavior. Without our frontal lobes, we wouldn't be able to plan, coordinate, control, and execute behavior. When we see, hear, touch, or taste something, the sensory information first heads to our brain's relay station located in the thalamus, which then relays sensory information to the frontal lobe. From there, it is sent to the center of the brain, known as the amygdala, which is responsible for producing the appropriate emotional response. However, when faced with a potentially threatening situation, the thalamus sends sensory information to both the frontal lobe and the amygdala at the same time. If the amygdala senses danger, it makes a split-second decision to initiate the fight-or-flight response before the frontal brain has time to overrule it. This cascade of events triggers the release of stress hormones, including adrenaline and cortisol. These hormones prepare our body to flee or fight by increasing our heart rate, elevating our blood pressure, and boosting our energy levels. However, emotional validation or acknowledgment—whether from someone else or from ourselves—helps prevent an amygdala-induced overreaction and returns us to our thinking brain.

REFLECTIONS

Where in your life are you experiencing a fight-or-flight response? Take a few moments to invite God's love into those places. How would a kind Heavenly Parent respond to you? Can you believe that God has that kind of compassion and grace for your frailties?

Suggested scripture reading for further study: Psalm 34:4-5, Isaiah 49:13, and Lamentations 3:22-23

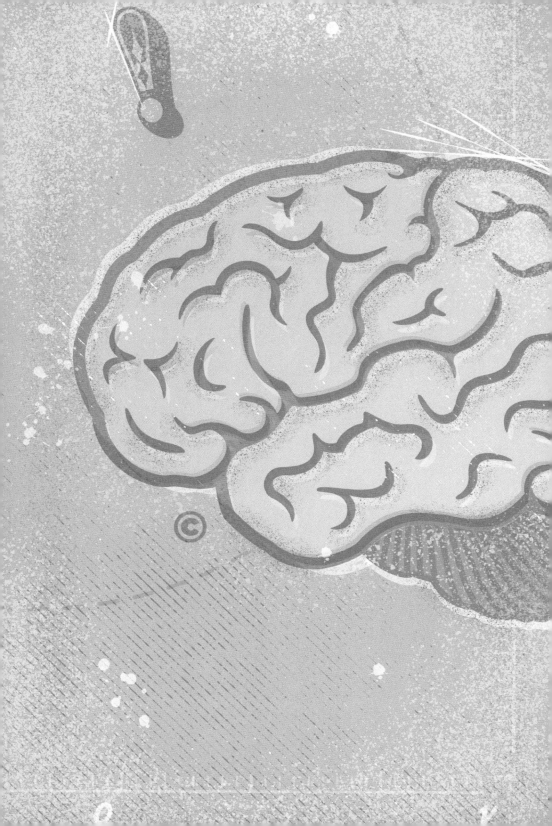

Day 26:
Fourth
Sunday *in* Lent

Pause from the devotion &
read *Psalm 104*

The LORD wraps himself in light as with
    a garment;
    he stretches out the heavens like a tent
    and lays the beams of his upper chambers
    on their waters.

He makes the clouds his chariot
    and rides on the wings of the wind.

He makes winds his messengers,
    flames of fire his servants.

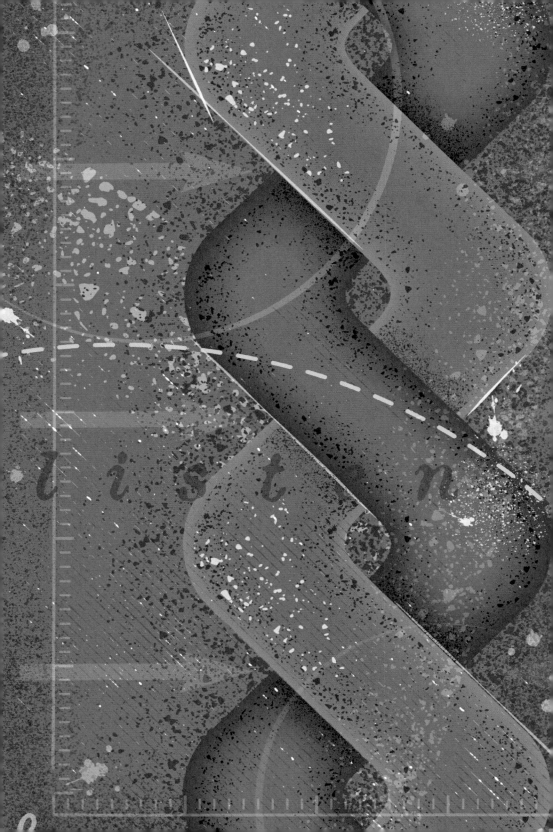

Day 27: Relationships

As we look at the scientifically proven actions that lead to broken relationships—criticism, defensiveness, contempt, and stonewalling—we can infer the opposite is true of healthy relationships. As an individual therapist, as well as a couples counselor, I know how important it is in our relationships with ourselves and with others to be accepting, listening, validating, and present. These seem to be the ingredients that relax a person's nervous system. Maybe that's why relationships have been proven to boost human performance. Research shows that people work better in teams. In 2009, researchers at Oxford University found that "team players can tolerate twice as much pain as those who work alone." In 2006, researchers at Harvard University found that heart surgeons' performance improves when they work with their standard team in their usual hospital. The New York Times unearthed some interesting information: "In a 2015 study, executives said that profitability increases when workers are persuaded to collaborate more.... If a company wants to outstrip its competitors, it needs to influence not only how people work but also how they work together." Collaboration, nurturance, and encouragement give us a dopamine boost that appears to help us better operate the problem-solving part of our brain. Relationships also increase our mental health. Suicide rates go down when people know they have even one person they can call at any time. Even God exists in the relationship of the Trinity. At the center of our Universe, there is a relationship.

REFLECTIONS

Research seems to show that knowing we are not alone is powerful for fueling our hope. How does knowing that Jesus is Emmanuel, which means "God with us," impact you? How can you give and receive the gift of being present with the people in your life, even if you can't change the challenges they face?

Suggested scripture reading for further study: Romans 15:13, Joshua 1:9, and Ecclesiastes 4:9-12

Day 28: Dung Beetles

Thank God for dung beetles! Without them, our planet would be covered in animal poop and, consequently, flies. Not to mention their burrowing of dung protects digested seeds by giving them a chance to germinate. Therefore, we'd also have fewer plants without these little pooper scoopers. There are three types of dung beetles: tunnelers, dwellers, and rollers. Tunnelers land on a manure pat and simply dig down into the pat, burying a portion of the dung. Dwellers are content with staying on top of the dung pat to lay their eggs and raise the young. Rollers form a bit of dung into a ball, roll it away, and bury it. Although all are helpful, the most entertaining to watch are the rollers. The male offers the female a giant-sized brood ball. If she accepts it, they roll it away together or the female may just ride on top of the ball. They must watch out though as other beetles may try to steal their ball! The new pair finds a soft place to bury the ball before mating. Whether they're rollers, tunnelers, or dwellers, they're mighty recyclers! By burying animal dung, the beetles loosen and nourish the soil and help control fly populations. The average domestic cow drops ten to twelve dung pats per day, and each pat can produce up to 3,000 flies within two weeks. In parts of Texas, dung beetles bury about eighty percent of cattle dung. If they didn't, the manure would harden, plants would die, and the pastureland would be a barren, smelly landscape filled with flies!

REFLECTIONS

It seems that details are important to God. In addition to creating a thriving living landscape, God remembered to manage waste. Imagine the Trinity, God three in one, filled with joy while creating our world, making sure each aspect continues the cycle of life. Spend some time thanking the Trinity for their creativity and thoroughness.

Suggested scripture reading for further study: Job 12:7-10 and Proverbs 30:24-27 (ESV)

Day 29:

Wind

Wind is air in motion, travelling between areas of different pressure. Air from high pressure areas moves toward areas of low pressure. The main differences in air pressure are caused by differences in temperature. When air heats up, the molecules rise and expand (low air pressure); when air cools, the molecules condense and sink toward the ground (high air pressure). Both warm air and cool air move up into the atmosphere, but because the warm air weighs less, it keeps pushing up through the cold air. This movement is wind. The sun provides heat to our planet, but it doesn't give the same amount of heat to the entire surface at the same time. Different land masses, plus the distance between the Earth's surface and the sun, create this uneven heat. In places where the sun's rays are more direct, the Earth is always warmer. This causes the flow of wind as there's more warm air pushing upward. If the Earth did not rotate and remained stationary, the atmosphere would circulate between the poles (high pressure areas) and the equator (low pressure area) in a simple back-and-forth pattern. But because the Earth rotates, circulating air is deflected (Coriolis force). Instead of circulating in a straight pattern, the air deflects toward the right in the Northern Hemisphere and toward the left in the Southern Hemisphere. Wind dries up soggy, wet areas and takes the water that doesn't absorb into the ground back up into the atmosphere. The wind also plays an important role in helping plants reproduce by carrying seeds to different parts of the ground to take root and grow and by carrying pollen from one plant to another so fruits, vegetables, and flowers can form.

REFLECTIONS

God has given us an atmosphere to ensure that air is not stagnate but continues to flow around the globe. Where is the wind of the Spirit blowing in your life? What might the Spirit be inviting you to see or do?

Day 30: Rocks

Rocks make up the outer crust of the Earth's surface. There are three major types of rocks: metamorphic, igneous, and sedimentary. Metamorphic rocks are formed by great heat and pressure. They are generally found inside the Earth's crust, where there is enough heat and pressure for them to form. Igneous rocks are formed by volcanoes. When a volcano erupts, it spews out hot molten rock called magma or lava. Eventually the magma will cool down and harden, either when it reaches the Earth's surface or somewhere within the crust. Sedimentary rocks are formed by the accumulation of sediments. Rocks are constantly changing in what is called the rock cycle. It takes millions of years for rocks to change. The rock cycle begins when melted rock or magma is sent to the Earth's surface by a volcano. It cools and forms an igneous rock. Next, the weather or a river and other events will slowly break up this rock into small pieces of sediment. As sediment builds up and hardens over the years, a sedimentary rock is formed. Slowly this sediment rock is covered by other rocks and ends up deep in the Earth's crust. When the pressure and heat get high enough, the sedimentary rock will metamorphose into a metamorphic rock, and the cycle will start over again.

REFLECTIONS

Recycling air, water, and even rock seems important to God. Why might God have created a system that reuses the same materials? In what ways does your life support this system or possibly disrupt this system? Where might God be calling you to be mindful in terms of this recycling system?

Suggested scripture reading for further study: Psalm 61:2-3 (ESV), Jeremiah 33:2-3, and Romans 12:12

Day 31: Grass

Grasses make up about twenty-six percent of the plant life on Earth and account for thirty percent of the world's land area. Varieties of grass grow on all continents, even in polar regions. Grasslands are found where there is not enough regular rainfall to support the growth of a forest, but not so little that a desert forms. In fact, grasslands often lie between forests and deserts. Grass is diverse and extremely important to most people's lives. For one thing, grass is a major food source all over the world. Rice, corn, and oats come from grass plants. Most livestock animals feed primarily on grasses. In some parts of the world, people use grass plants like bamboo in construction. Giant bamboo, which can grow up to 151 feet tall, is the largest variety of grass. Grass is also used to make sugar, liquor, and bread, among many other things. Wherever it grows, grass plays a vital role in curbing erosion. Embedded plant materials not only reinforce soils, but also act as barriers to soil movement, moisture wicks, and hydraulic drains. Grasses, like all other plants, produce the oxygen we breathe through photosynthesis.

REFLECTIONS

Grass exists on all continents. Although many ecosystems grow specific plants to their regions, it's interesting that grass exists in all ecosystems. It seems like a foundational organism for life. When you see grass today, consider your fellow human beings and the grass in their landscapes. Consider all that you have in common. As you think about this, how might your love and prayers extend to all people?

Suggested scripture reading for further study: Ephesians 6:18, 1 John 4:7, and Hebrews 12:14

Day 32:

Love

Lust is governed by both estrogen and testosterone in both men and women. Attraction is driven by adrenaline, dopamine, and serotonin—the same chemicals that are released by exciting, novel experiences. Long-term attachment is governed by a very different set of hormones and brain chemicals: oxytocin and vasopressin, which encourage bonding. Interestingly, oxytocin is known as the cuddle hormone and is the hormone that drives the bond between mother and child. Each of these chemicals works in a specific part of the brain to influence the three stages of romantic relationships: lust, attraction, and attachment. During the initial stages of lust and attraction, the neurotransmitter releases the chemicals that send people into that love-struck phase that often causes them to think of nothing else but this new person in their life, not unlike our brain's response to addiction. As a result, people may even lose their appetite and their sleep during this stage. The longest our brains can produce this type of high is eighteen to twenty-four months. If this didn't have a limited shelf life, humanity wouldn't be very productive. In the next phase, when attachment hormones set in, they create a warm, comforting feeling. These hormones are often reinforced when people receive attention through their particular love language: words, time, service, gifts, or physical affection. Attachment is the predominant factor in all long-term relationships. Whereas lust and attraction are exclusive to romantic relationships, attachment mediates all other relationships.

Suggested scripture reading for further study: Psalm 103: 11, Romans 12:15 (ESV), and 1 Corinthians 13

REFLECTIONS

The Trinity exists in communion with each other. We as humans, made in God's image, were made for connection too, and our bodies are designed to reinforce that connection. How can you cultivate connection with those around you, whether with family or friends? You can't touch God, but what practices help you feel most connected to God? How can you make space for those practices?

Day 33:
Fifth Sunday in Lent

Palm Sunday
Pause from the devotion & read *Psalm 65*

The grasslands of the wilderness overflow;

the hills are clothed with gladness.

The meadows are covered with flocks

and the valleys are mantled with grain;

they shout for joy and sing.

Day 34: Soil

Soil is fundamentally from bedrock. Soil is what covers most of the land on Earth; it's the uppermost layer of the crust. It is why plants and trees can stay anchored to the ground. This layer provides a home for insects, worms, and other burrowing animals. Soil is formed over long periods of time. It can take up to 1,000 years to form just an inch of soil. The parent material, which is generally a huge rock, breaks down into smaller pieces through the actions of rain, frost, heat, and wind. Over time, green moss and tiny plants slowly grow on the smaller pieces of rocks. This initial vegetation dies, and the remains of these dead plants make room for larger plants. This process continues to break down the rock until soil is formed. This breaking down allows the rock's minerals to become available for plants and, in this form, it's also able to hold water, which is essential for life. The sequence of development creates layers in soil: topsoil, subsoil, and bedrock. Rich in organic matter, topsoil is where seeds germinate and many living organisms like worms and fungus are found. Subsoil is harder and carries fewer minerals. Below the subsoil lies bedrock, or the parent rock, which contains no organic matter. The common gardening soil you purchase at the hardware store takes thousands of years to come to fruition.

REFLECTIONS

Decay is important for the nutrient value of the soil. How have little deaths in your life become nutrient seed beds for something new? Or do these places of hardship and suffering feel void of any possibility? If so, are you willing to converse with God about those places and ask for new life in those areas?

Suggested scripture reading for further study: John 15:1-8, Matthew 13:5-9, and 2 Corinthians 4:15-17

Layer A.

Layer B.

Layer C.

Layer D.

Layer E

Day 35:

Desert

Found on every continent, deserts cover more than one-fifth of the Earth's land area. Primarily defined by their lack of rain, deserts generally receive ten inches or less rain in a year. They are so dry that sometimes rain evaporates before it can hit the ground! Because deserts are so dry and their humidity is so low, they have no blanket to help insulate the ground. As a result, they may get very hot during the day but don't hold the heat overnight. Some deserts can reach temperatures of well over 100°F during the day and then drop below freezing during the night. As the equator receives the most sunlight throughout the year, it's fair to presume that equatorial regions should also be the hottest. Interestingly, that's not the case. The hottest parts of the world are not located near the equator, but rather around the tropics. The equator gets the most sunlight, but a good portion of this sunlight is used up in evaporating water from seas and other water bodies. This results in the formation of moist, warm air over equatorial oceans, which then begins to rise and form clouds. This warm air unloads almost all of its moisture in the clouds above equatorial regions but still continues to move higher up. This warm air, now also dry, begins to move toward the pole, but is stopped due to the Coriolis force, which prevents it from continuing in the direction of the poles. As a result, it loops back closer to the surface in the tropics, creating the hot, dry conditions needed to form deserts.

REFLECTIONS

When the stressors of life have absorbed all the moisture from your being, how do you respond to God? Maybe you have arid places in you right now. If so, take time to ask God to help you in these arid places. If you run out of words, allow Jesus (who has experience with what it feels like to have a parched soul) to be with you.

Suggested scripture reading for further study: Psalm 63:1, Jeremiah 17:8, and Isaiah 49:10

Day 36:

Sand

Much of the world's sand is made up of tiny crystals of the mineral quartz. Quartz is made out of silicone and oxygen, the two most common elements in the Earth's crust. Quartz grains are small and really tough. Quartz forms within a cooling blob of molten granite rock or magma deep under the Earth's surface. As the magma cools, different minerals crystalize into solid rock at different temperatures. Quartz is one of the last minerals to form. It's forced to crystalize in the tiny spaces left in between the other hardened minerals in the cooling rock. This has a benefit. Minerals that form in the hotter conditions have weaker chemical structures and weather more easily with wind, rain, and freezing/thawing cycles. As the weak minerals wear away, the unfaltering quartz grains pop out of the rock as sand. The quartz sand is whisked away by streams and rivers and carried out to sea. At the mouth of the river, the fast-flowing water slows abruptly, and the well-rounded sand drops out. Larger rocks and pebbles are left upstream whereas smaller sediments, like silt and clay, continue to be swept along by the weaker current and are deposited further from the shore. Over thousands of years, the paths of rivers sweep up and down the coast, dropping off piles of sand to be spread by waves and currents into smooth sandy beaches.

REFLECTIONS

One function of sand is that it acts as a barrier preventing coastal erosion from powerful waves. The accumulation of this sand develops through pressure, both in its formation and its travel. How are you formed in times of adversity? What particles in your life, like sand, are evidence of God's work in adversity?

Suggested scripture reading for further study: Psalm 139:17-18, Jeremiah 5:22 (ESV), James 1:2-4, and 2 Corinthians 12:9

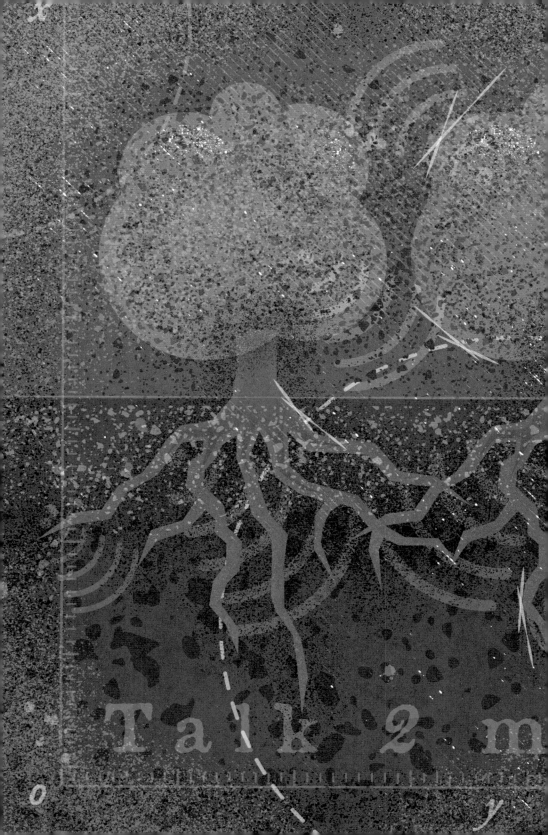

Day 37:
Plants Communicate
with Each Other

Plants communicate with each other using both above- and below-ground channels. According to ecologist Richard Karban, "When plant leaves get damaged, whether by hungry insects or an invading lawn mower, they release plumes of volatile chemicals. They're what's responsible for the smell of freshly cut grass." A study at the University of Aberdeen revealed that, when aphids devour lima bean leaves, the leaves not only emit an odor that attracts aphid-eating wasps but they also send signals through fungus in the soil. Plants are also sensitive enough to discern between general touch and when they're being eaten by insects. Chemical compounds found in the insect's saliva help the plant make that distinction. For some plants, like sage brush, when they receive the distress signals from their neighbors, they adjust their own internal chemistry, creating an insect repellent. When it comes to touch, plant communication also helps other plants navigate crowded conditions. According to a Swedish University study, when plants receive communication from other plants about the location of their neighbors, they modify their growth behavior accordingly.

REFLECTIONS

Communication seems important to God. What does this stir in you as you consider God developing this relational layer into vegetation? Plants share information about their challenges in order to benefit others. How can you share what you are learning as an offering to someone who might benefit and be encouraged by it? Also consider how you can learn from others.

Suggested scripture reading for further study: Psalm 96:12, 2 Corinthians 1:3-4, and 1 Peter 3:15

Day 38: Hummingbirds

Hummingbirds have long intrigued scientists. Their wings can beat seventy times a second. Their hearts can beat more than 1,000 times a minute. They live on nectar and can pack on forty percent of their body weight in fat for migration. Hummingbirds are the fighter pilots of the avian world, diving and weaving at speeds of up to fifty-five kilometers per hour—then turning on a dime to hover midair, wings frantically beating, as they refuel on nectar. Hummingbirds drink nectar using tongues that are so long that, when retracted, they coil up inside the birds' heads, around their skulls and eyes. At its tip, the tongue divides in two, and its outer edges curve inward, creating two tubes running side by side. Many North American hummingbird species are migratory, covering enormous distances each year as they journey between summer breeding grounds in the north and overwintering areas in the south. The pugnacious Rufous Hummingbird travels roughly 3,900 miles (one way). Traveling in an enormous loop, it moves northward along the Pacific Coast from wintering sites in Mexico to summer breeding grounds as far north as Alaska. At about 2.25 inches long and weighing 0.07 ounces, the Bee Hummingbird is the smallest living bird in the world.

REFLECTIONS

What was the response within the Trinity when they conceived these impressive acrobatic fliers? Was it exhilarating? Did it spark joy, laughter, and delight? What prompted them to create not just one hummingbird, but a variety of these tiny hovering birds? What feelings well up in you when you see these tiny hovering birds?

Suggested scripture reading for further study: Matthew 6:26, Jeremiah 10:12, and Romans 1:20

hum

Day 39: Giving

Scientists have discovered that, when volunteers placed the interests of others before their own, the generosity activated a primitive part of the brain that usually lights up in response to food or sex. Donating affects two brain reward systems working together: the midbrain VTA, which also is stimulated by food, sex, drugs and money, and the subgenual area, which is stimulated when humans see babies and romantic partners. In one study, people with multiple sclerosis were trained to provide support over the telephone for fifteen minutes a month to a fellow person with multiple sclerosis. The helpers proved to be more self-confident, had better self-esteem, and displayed less depression. In a similar study, people with chronic pain who counseled those with similar conditions experienced a drop in their own symptoms of pain and depression. In a study of alcoholics going through the Alcoholics Anonymous program, those who helped others were nearly twice as likely to stay sober a year later, and their levels of depression were lower, too. Experts call this the "wounded healer" principle. Helping has a tremendous benefit for those who need it as well as for the helpers themselves.

REFLECTIONS

Consider the kindnesses you have received from God, especially the gift of this world. Maybe you feel grateful for the air you breathe, the food you eat, the water you drink, and even the temperature regulated through the atmospheric system. Consider the many layers of creation that support these gifts, such as soil, rocks, the Moon, plankton, dung beetles, and honey bees, along with all the other big and small parts of creation that allow life here on Earth. In what ways can you reflect this kindness from God to others and the world? Does this feel overwhelming or life giving? Do you possibly need help from the Creator to spark your imagination? Spend some time inviting God to creatively reflect that kindness through you out into the world as your gift back to God.

Suggested scripture reading for further study: 2 Corinthians 9:11, Proverbs 11:24-25, and Proverbs 18:16

Day 40:

Sixth Sunday in Lent

Easter
Read *Psalm 148*

Praise the LORD from the earth,

you great sea creatures and all ocean depths,

lightning and hail, snow and clouds,

stormy winds that do his bidding,

you mountains and all hills,

fruit trees and all cedars,

wild animals and all cattle,

small creatures and flying birds,

kings of the earth and all nations,

you princes and all rulers on earth,

young men and women,

old people and children.

Easter is our recognition that death has been conquered. The tomb is empty; Christ is risen! We understand that, through Jesus' death and resurrection, we're ushered into a new era that allows us to come into direct relationship with God. As you celebrate this good news, consider creating for yourself a type of celebration for today that incorporates your gratefulness for the world in which God has invited you to live. Is there a favorite devotional topic that you want to explore further? Maybe it's a quiet celebration by a lake to notice plankton and thank God for the air you breathe. Or maybe you want to create a dinner party using honey bees as your theme.

Where is Jesus in this celebration, you ask? Well, consider the beginning of John's Gospel as it opens with a description of Jesus.

"In the beginning was the Word, and the Word was with God, and the Word was God. He was with God in the beginning. Through Him, all things were made; without him nothing was made that has been made."

Enjoy your celebration as you think about God speaking creation into life.

Acknowledgments

I want to thank my team of family and friends who helped weave this book together. My middle daughter, Annabelle, asked me most days, "What's the topic today, Mom?" and then eagerly ate up the science details and pondered these wonders with me. My oldest daughter, Alex, shared her copy-editing skills, which helped me tidy up the initial manuscript so I could share it with friends. Audrey, my youngest, gently teased me about my obsessions and then genuinely asked questions about the Big and Small. My artist husband, Kory, has encouraged creative living across all aspects of life; his visual partnership breathed another dimension into this project. Then there's my insightful team of readers. What a joy and privilege to have so many spiritually thoughtful and scholarly women in my life who were willing to give this devotion its test run! Your feedback has been invaluable! Thank you, Libby Chapman, Katie Cross, Katie Eilers, Kathy Keith, Patra Mueller, and Alisa Prinos.

Scriptures

Day 1 Stars
He determines the number of the stars and calls them each by name. Great is our Lord and mighty in power; his understanding has no limit. **Psalm 147:4-5**

The Heavens declare the glory of God; the skies proclaim the work of his hands. **Psalm 19:1**

The LORD your God is in your midst, a mighty one who will save; he will rejoice over you with gladness; he will quiet you by his love; he will exult over you with loud singing. **Zephaniah 3:17 (ESV)**

Day 2 Particles
Great are the works of the Lord; they are pondered by all who delight in them. **Psalm 111:2**

Lord, you have been our dwelling place throughout all generations. Before the mountains were born or you brought forth the whole world, from everlasting to everlasting you are God. **Psalm 90:1-2**

"I am the Alpha and the Omega," says the Lord God, "who is, and who was, and who is to come, the Almighty." **Revelation 1:8**

Day 3 Smiles
The LORD bless you and keep you; the LORD make his face shine on you and be gracious to you; the LORD turn his face toward you and give you peace. **Numbers 6:24-26**

A cheerful heart is good medicine, but a crushed spirit dries up the bones. **Proverbs 17:22**

Day 4 Cherry Blossoms
By the seventh day God had finished the work he had been doing; so on the seventh day he rested from all his work. **Genesis 2:2**

Come to me, all you who are weary and burdened, and I will give you rest. Take my yoke upon you and learn from me, for I am gentle and humble in heart, and you will find rest for your souls. For my yoke is easy and my burden is light. **Matthew 11:28-30**

Being confident of this, that he who began a good work in you will carry it on to completion until the day of Christ Jesus. **Philippians 1:6**

Day 5, First Sunday in Lent—Genesis 1

Day 6 Honey Bees
There are different kinds of gifts, but the same Spirit distributes them. There are different kinds of service, but the same Lord. There are different kinds of working, but in all of them and in everyone it is the same God at work. **1 Corinthians 12: 4-6**

Whether you turn to the right or to the left, your ears will hear a voice behind you, saying, "This is the way; walk in it." **Isaiah 30:21**

Know also that wisdom is like honey for you: If you find it, there is a future hope for you, and your hope will not be cut off. **Proverbs 24:14**

Day 7 Tectonic Plates

God is our refuge and strength, an ever-present help in trouble. Therefore we will not fear, though the earth give way and the mountains fall into the heart of the sea, though its waters roar and foam and the mountains quake with their surging. **Psalm 46: 1-3**

My flesh and my heart may fail, but God is the strength of my heart and my portion forever. **Psalm 73:26**

Jesus Christ is the same yesterday and today and forever. **Hebrews 13:8**

Day 8 Plankton

How many are your works, Lord! In wisdom you made them all; the earth is full of your creatures. There is the sea, vast and spacious, teeming with creatures beyond number—living things both large and small. **Psalm 104:24-25**

And my God will meet all your needs according to the riches of his glory in Christ Jesus. **Philippians 4:19**

Let everything that has breath praise the LORD. **Psalm 150:6**

Day 9 Bag Bugs

But you, Lord, are a shield around me, my glory, the One who lifts my head high. **Psalm 3:3**

My salvation and my honor depend on God; he is my mighty rock, my refuge. Trust in him at all times, you people; pour out your hearts to him, for God is your refuge. **Psalm 62:7-8**

One thing I ask from the LORD, this only do I seek: that I may dwell in the house of the LORD all the days of my life, to gaze on the beauty of the LORD and to seek him in his temple. For in the day of trouble he will keep me safe in his dwelling; he will hide me in the shelter of his sacred tent and set me high upon a rock. **Psalm 27:4-5**

Day 10 Immune System

For you created my inmost being; you knit me together in my mother's womb. I praise you because I am fearfully and wonderfully made; your works are wonderful. I know that full well. **Psalms 139: 13-14**

He heals the brokenhearted and binds up their wounds. **Psalm 147:3**

And the God of all grace, who called you to his eternal glory in Christ, after you have suffered a little while, will himself restore you and make you strong, firm and stead-fast. **1 Peter 5:10**

Day 11 Clouds

The Lord wraps himself in light as with a garment; he stretches out the heavens like a tent and lays the beams of his upper chambers on their waters. He makes the clouds his chariot and rides on the wings of the wind. **Psalm 104:2-4**

Sing to the Lord with grateful praise; make music to our God on the harp. He covers the sky with clouds; he supplies the earth with rain and makes grass grow on the hills. **Psalm 147:7-8**

But whoever drinks the water I give them will never thirst. Indeed, the water I give them will become in them a spring of water welling up to eternal life. **John 4:14**

Day 12, Second Sunday in Lent—Psalm 139

Day 13 Douglas Fir Trees

So that there should be no division in the body, but that its parts should have equal concern for each other. If one part suffers, every part suffers with it; if one part is honored, every part rejoices with it. Now you are the body of Christ, and each one of you is a part of it. **1 Corinthians 12:25-27**

Carry each other's burdens, and in this way you will fulfill the law of Christ. **Galatians 6:2**

Day 14 Animal Heart Beats

Above all else, guard your heart, for everything you do flows from it. **Proverbs 4:23**.

Whoever does not love, does not love God, because God is love. **1 John 4:8**

You did not choose me, but I chose you and appointed you so that you might go and bear fruit—fruit that will last—and so that whatever you ask in my name the Father will give you. This is my command: Love each other. **John 15:16-17**

Day 15 North/South Axis

All this I have spoken while still with you. But the Advocate, the Holy Spirit, whom the Father will send in my name, will teach you all things and will remind you of everything I have said to you. **John 14:25-26**

In the same way, the Spirit helps us in our weakness. We do not know what we ought to pray for, but the Spirit himself intercedes for us through wordless groans. And he who searches our hearts knows the mind of the Spirit, because the Spirit intercedes for God's people in accordance with the will of God. **Romans 8:26-27**

Day 16 Size of the Universe

He determines the number of the stars and calls them each by name. Great is our Lord and mighty in power; his understanding has no limit. **Psalm 147:4-5**

For as high as the heavens are above the earth, so great is his love for those who fear him. As far as the east is from the west, so far has he removed our transgressions from us. **Psalm 103:11-12**

The God who made the world and everything in it is the Lord of heaven and earth and does not live in temples built by human hands. And he is not served by human hands, as if he needed anything. Rather, he himself gives everyone life and breath and everything else. From one man he made all the nations, that they should inhabit the whole earth; and he marked out their appointed times in history and the boundaries of their lands. God did this so that they would seek him and perhaps reach out for him and find him, though he is not far from any one of us. 'For in him we live and move and have our being.' As some of your own poets have said, 'We are his offspring.' **Acts 17:24-28**

Day 17 Math

He is before all things, and in him all things hold together. **Colossians 1:17**

Why do you call me, 'Lord, Lord,' and do not do what I say? As for everyone who comes to me and hears my words and puts them into practice, I will show you what they are like. They are like a man building a house, who dug down deep and laid the foundation on rock. When a flood came, the torrent struck that house but could not shake it, because it was well built. **Luke 6:46-48**

Day 18 Sunflowers

Let the fields be jubilant, and everything in them; let all the trees of the forest sing for joy. Let all creation rejoice before the Lord. **Psalm 96:12-13a**

Finally, brothers and sisters, whatever is true, whatever is noble, whatever is right, whatever is pure, whatever is lovely, whatever is admirable—if anything is excellent or praiseworthy—think about such things. **Philippians 4:8**

Your word is a lamp for my feet, a light on my path. **Psalm 119:105**

Day 19, Third Sunday in Lent—Psalm 96

Day 20 Moon

And God said, "Let there be lights in the vault of the sky to separate the day from the night, and let them serve as signs to mark sacred times, and days and years, and let them be lights in the vault of the sky to give light on the earth." And it was so. God made two great lights—the greater light to govern the day and the lesser light to govern the night. He also made the stars. God set them in the vault of the sky to give light on the earth, to govern the day and the night, and to separate light from darkness. And God saw that it was good. And there was evening, and there was morning—the fourth day.**Genesis 1:14-19**

He made the moon to mark the seasons, and the sun knows when to go down. **Psalm 104:19**

Are you tired? Worn out? Burned out on religion? Come to me. Get away with me and you'll recover your life. I'll show you how to take a real rest. Walk with me and work with me—watch how I do it. Learn the unforced rhythms of grace. I won't lay anything heavy or ill-fitting on you. Keep company with me and you'll learn to live freely and lightly. **Matthew 11:28-30 (MSG)**

Day 21 Magnetic Field

He set the earth on its foundations; it can never be moved. **Psalm 104:5**

But you, GOD, shield me on all sides; You ground my feet, you lift my head high; With all my might I shout up to GOD, His answers thunder from the holy mountain. **Psalm 3:3-4 (MSG)**

Every word of God is flawless; he is a shield to those who take refuge in him. **Proverbs 30:5**

Day 22 Hippos

He makes springs pour water into the ravines, it flows between the mountains. They give water to all the beasts of the field; the wild donkeys quench their thirst. The birds of the sky nest by the waters; they sing among the branches. He waters the mountains from his upper chambers; the land is satisfied by the fruit of his work. He makes grass grow for the cattle, and plants for people to cultivate—bringing forth food from the earth. **Psalm 104:10-14**

For just as each of us has one body with many members, and these members do not all have the same function, so in Christ we, though many, form one body, and each member belongs to all the others. **Romans 12:4-5**

And over all these virtues put on love, which binds them all together in perfect unity. Let the peace of Christ rule in your hearts, since as members of one body you were called to peace. And be thankful. Let the message of Christ dwell among you

Day 22 Hippos (con't)

richly as you teach and admonish one another with all wisdom through psalms, hymns, and songs from the Spirit, singing to God with gratitude in your hearts. Colossians 3:14-16

Day 23 Light

If I say, "Surely the darkness will hide me and the light become night around me," even the darkness will not be dark to you; the night will shine like the day, for darkness is as light to you. Psalm 139:11-12

When Jesus spoke again to the people, he said, "I am the light of the world. Whoever follows me will never walk in darkness, but will have the light of life." John 8:12

This, in essence, is the message we heard from Christ and are passing on to you: God is light, pure light; there's not a trace of darkness in him. If we claim that we experience a shared life with him and continue to stumble around in the dark, we're obviously lying through our teeth—we're not living what we claim. But if we walk in the light, God himself being the light, we also experience a shared life with one another, as the sacrificed blood of Jesus, God's Son, purges all our sin. If we claim that we're free of sin, we're only fool-ing ourselves. A claim like that is errant nonsense. On the other hand, if we admit our sins—make a clean breast of them—he won't let us down; he'll be true to himself. He'll forgive our sins and purge us of all wrongdoing. If we claim that we've never sinned, we out-and-out contradict God—make a liar out of him. A claim like that only shows off our ignorance of God. 1 John 1:5-9 (MSG)

Day 24 Leaves

Then God said, "Let the land produce vegetation: seed-bearing plants and trees on the land that bear fruit with seed in it, according to their various kinds." And it was so. The land produced vegetation: plants bearing seed according to their kinds and trees bearing fruit with seed in it according to their kinds. And God saw that it was good. And there was evening, and there was morning—the third day. Genesis 1:11-13

Day 25 Frontal Lobe of the Human Brain

I sought the Lord, and he answered me; he delivered me from all my fears. Those who look to him are radiant; their faces are never covered with shame. Psalm 34:4-5

Shout for joy, you heavens; rejoice, you earth; burst into song, you mountains! For the LORD comforts his people and will have compassion on his afflicted ones. Isaiah 49:13

Because of the LORD's great love we are not consumed, for his compassions never fail. They are new every morning; great is your faithfulness. Lamentations 3:22-23

Day 26, Fourth Sunday in Lent—Psalm 104

Day 27 Relationships

May the God of hope fill you with all joy and peace as you trust in him, so that you may overflow with hope by the power of the Holy Spirit. Romans 15:13

Have I not commanded you? Be strong and courageous. Do not be afraid; do not be discouraged, for the LORD your God will be with you wherever you go. Joshua 1:9

Day 27 Relationships (con't)

Two are better than one; because they have a good return for their labor: If either of them falls down, one can help the other up. But pity anyone who falls and has no one to help them up. Also, if two lie down together, they will keep warm. But how can one keep warm alone? Though one may be overpowered, two can defend themselves. A cord of three strands is not quickly broken. **Ecclesiastes 4:9-12**

Day 28 Dung Beetles

But ask the animals, and they will teach you, or the birds in the sky, and they will tell you; or speak to the earth, and it will teach you, or let the fish in the sea inform you. Which of all these does not know that the hand of the LORD has done this? In his hand is the life of every creature and the breath of all mankind. **Job 12:7-10**

Four things on earth are small, but they are exceedingly wise the ants are a people not strong men yet they provide their food in the summer; the rock badgers are a people not mighty, yet they make their homes in the cliffs; the locusts have no king, yet all of them march in rank; the lizard you can take in your hands, yet it is in kings' palaces. **Proverbs 30: 24-27 (ESV)**

Day 29 Wind

When the Spirit of truth comes, he will guide you into all the truth, for he will not speak on his own authority, but whatever he hears he will speak, and he will declare to you the things that are to come. **John 16:13**

Show me your ways, LORD, teach me your paths. Guide me in your truth and teach me, for you are God my Savior, and my hope is in you all day long. **Psalm 25:4-5**

Day 30 Rocks

Lead me to the rock that is higher than I. For you have been my refuge, a strong tower against the enemy. **Psalm 61:2-3 (ESV)**

This is what the Lord says, he who made the earth, the Lord who formed it and established it—the Lord is his name: 'call to me and I will answer you and tell you great and unsearchable things you do not know.' **Jeremiah 33:2-3**

Be joyful in hope, patient in affliction, faithful in prayer. **Romans 12:12**

Day 31 Grass

And pray in the Spirit on all occasions with all kinds of prayers and requests. With this in mind, be alert and always keep on praying for all the Lord's people. **Ephesians 6:18**

Dear friends, let us love one another, for love comes from God. Everyone who loves has been born of God and knows God. **1 John 4:7**

Make every effort to live in peace with everyone and to be holy; without holiness no one will see the Lord. **Hebrews 12:14**

Day 32 Love

For as high as the heavens are above the earth, so great is his steadfast love toward us. **Psalm 103:11**

Rejoice with those who rejoice, weep with those who weep.
Romans 12:15 (ESV)

1 Corinthians 13

Day 33, Fifth Sunday in Lent—Psalm 65

Day 34 Soil

I am the true vine, and my Father is the gardener. He cuts off every branch in me that bears no fruit, while every branch that does bear fruit he prunes so that it will be even more fruitful. You are already clean because of the word I have spoken to you. Remain in me, as I also remain in you. No branch can bear fruit by itself; it must remain in the vine. Neither can you bear fruit unless you remain in me. I am the vine; you are the branches. If you remain in me and I in you, you will bear much fruit; apart from me you can do noth-ing. If you do not remain in me, you are like a branch that is thrown away and withers; such branches are picked up, thrown into the fire and burned. If you remain in me and my words remain in you, ask whatever you wish, and it will be done for you. This is to my Father's glory, that you bear much fruit, showing yourselves to be my disciples. John 15:1-8

Other seeds fell on rocky ground, where they did not have much soil, and imme-diately they sprang up, since they had no depth of soil, but when the sun rose they were scorched. And since they had no root, they withered away. Other seeds fell among thorns, and the thorns grew up and choked them. Other seeds fell on good soil and produced grain, some a hundredfold, some sixty, some thirty. He who has ears, let him hear. Matthew 13:5-9

For it is all for your sake, so that as grace extends to more and more people it may increase thanksgiving, to the glory of God. So we do not lose heart. Though our outer self is wasting away, our inner self is being renewed day by day. For this light momentary affliction is preparing for us an eternal weight of glory beyond all com-parison. 2 Corinthians 4:15-17

Day 35 Desert

You, God, are my God, earnestly I seek you; I thirst for you, my whole being longs for you, in a dry and parched land where there is no water. Psalm 63:1

They will be like a tree planted by the water that sends out its roots by the stream. It does not fear when heat comes; its leaves are always green. It has no worries in a year of drought and never fails to bear fruit. Jeremiah 17:8

They will neither hunger nor thirst, nor will the desert heat or the sun beat down on them. He who has compassion on them will guide them and lead them beside springs of water. Isaiah 49:10

Day 36 Sand

How precious to me are your thoughts, God! How vast is the sum of them! Were I to count them, they would outnumber the grains of sand—when I awake, I am still with you. Psalm 139:17-18

"Do you not fear me?" declares the Lord. "Do you not tremble before me? I placed the sand as the boundary for the sea, a perpetual barrier that it cannot pass; though the waves toss, they cannot prevail; though they roar, they cannot pass over it." Jeremiah 5:22 (ESV)

Consider it pure joy, my brothers and sisters, whenever you face trials of many kinds, because you know that the testing of your faith produces perseverance. Let perseverance finish its work so that you may be mature and complete, not lacking anything. James 1:2-4

Day 36 Sand (con't)

But he said to me, "My grace is sufficient for you, for my power is made perfect in weakness." Therefore I will boast all the more gladly about my weaknesses, so that Christ's power may rest on me. **2 Corinthians 12:9**

Day 37 Plant Communication

Let the fields be jubilant, and everything in them; let all the trees of the forest sing for joy. **Psalm 96:12**

Praise be to the God and Father of our Lord Jesus Christ, the Father of compassion and the God of all comfort, who comforts us in all our troubles, so that we can comfort those in any trouble with the comfort we ourselves receive from God. **2 Corinthians 1:3-4**

But in your hearts revere Christ as Lord. Always be prepared to give an answer to everyone who asks you to give the reason for the hope that you have. But do this with gentleness and respect. **1 Peter 3:15**

Day 38 Hummingbirds

Look at the birds of the air: they neither sow nor reap nor gather into barns, and yet your heavenly Father feeds them. Are you not of more value than they? **Matthew 6:26**

But God made the earth by his power; he founded the world by his wisdom and stretched out the heavens by his understanding. **Jeremiah 10:12**

For since the creation of the world God's invisible qualities—his eternal power and divine nature—have been clearly seen, being understood from what has been made, so that people are without excuse. **Romans 1:20**

Day 39 Giving

You will be enriched in every way so that you can be generous on every occasion, and through us your generosity will result in thanksgiving to God. **2 Corinthians 9:11**

One person gives freely, yet gains even more; another withholds unduly, but comes to poverty. A generous person will prosper; whoever refreshes others will be refreshed. **Proverbs 11:24-25**

A gift opens the way and ushers the giver into the presence of the great. **Proverbs 18:16**

Day 40, Sixth Sunday in Lent—Psalm 148

Sources

Stars

Masetti, Maggie. "How Many Stars in the Milky Way?" Nasa.gov, 22 July 2015, https://asd.gsfc.nasa.gov/blueshift/index php/2015/07/22/how-many-stars-in-the-milky-way/

Nagarja, Mamta Patel. "Stars." Nasa Science, Nasa.gov, 11 September 2020, https://science.nasa.gov/astrophysics/focus-areas/how-do-stars-form-and-evolve

Particles

Mann, Adam. "What are Elementary Particles?" Livescience.com, Future US, Inc., 7 May 2019, https://www.livescience.com/65427-fundamental-elementary-particles.html

"Particles of Matter Definition." Generationgenius.com, National Science Teachers Association, 2020, https://www.generationge-nius.com/particles-of-matter-lesson-for-kids/

"Simple Particle Theory: Lesson for Kids." Study.com, 8 April 2019, study.com/academy/lesson/simple-particle-theory-lesson-for-kids.html

Smiles

Savitz, Eric. "The Untapped Power of Smiling." Forbes.com, 12 September 2010, https://www.forbes.com/sites/ericsavitz/2011/03/22/the-untapped-power-of-smiling/#29f275777a67

Venton, Danielle. "Our Social Nature: The Surprising Science of Smiles." Wired.com, Conde Nast Productions, 19 August 2011, https://www.wired.com/2011/08/science-behind-smiles/

Cherry Blossoms

Ellis, Mary Ellen. "Cherry Cold Requirements: How Many Chill Hours for Cherries." Gardeningknowhow.com, 24, September 2018, https://www.gardeningknow-how.com/edible/fruits/cherry/chill-hours-for-cherries.htm

Palmer, Brian. "What Makes the Cherry Trees Bloom When They Do?" Washington-post.com, 4 April 2011, https://www.washingtonpost.com/national/what-makes-the-cherry-trees-bloom-when-they-do/2011/03/29/AFvRbRfC_story.html

Honey Bees

"What's the Waggle Dance? And Why Do Honeybees Do It?" Smithsonianmag.com www.smithsonianmag.com/videos/category/science/whats-the-waggle-dance-and-why-do-honeybees-do-it/

"The Waggle Dance of the Honey Bee." Youtube.com, Georgia Tech University, 2 February 2011, https://www.youtube.com/watch?v=bFDGPgXtK-U

Tectonic Plates

"Plate Tectonics." Nationalgeographic.com, https://www.nationalgeographic.com/science/earth/the-dynamic-earth/plate-tectonics/

Boyle, Rebecca. "Why Earth's Cracked Crust is Essential for Life." Quantamagazine.org, 7 June 2018, https://www.quantamagazine.org/plate-tectonics-may-be-essential-for-life-20180607/

Tectonic Plates (con't)

"What is Tectonic Shift." Oceanservicenoaa.gov, https://oceanservice.noaa.gov/facts/tectonics.html

Plankton

"What are Plankton." Oceanservice.noaa.gov, https://oceanservice.noaa.gov/facts/plankton.html

"What are Fossil Fuels?" Ocean.si.edu, Smithsonian National Museum of Natural History, https://ocean.si.edu/conservation/gulf-oil-spill/what-are-fossil-fuels

"How Much Oxygen Comes from the Ocean?" Oceanservice.noaa.gov, https://oceanservice.noaa.gov/facts/ocean-oxygen.html

Bag Bugs

Patowary, Kaushik. "Log House Like Cocoon of the Bagworm Moth." Amusingplanet.com, 29 January 2016, https://www.amusingplanet.com/2016/01/log-house-like-cocoon-of-bagworm-moth.html

Immune System

"Biology for Kids: Immune System." Ducksters.com, Technological Solutions Inc., https://www.ducksters.com/science/biology/immune_system.php

Bryce, Emma. "How Does Your Immune System Work?" Youtube.com, TedEd, 8 January 2018, https://www.youtube.com/watch?v=PSRJfaAYkW4

Clouds

"How Much Does a Cloud Weigh?" USGS.gov, https://www.usgs.gov/special-topic/water-science-school/science/how-much-does-a-cloud-weigh?

"Earth Science for Kids: Weather—Clouds." Ducksters.com, Technological Solutions Inc., https://www.ducksters.com/science/earth_science/clouds.php

"Clouds." Weatherwizkids.com, https://www.weatherwizkids.com/weather-clouds.htm

Douglas Fir Trees

"Douglas Fir." Nwf.org, The National Wildlife Federation, https://www.nwf.org/Educational-Resources/Wildlife-Guide/Plants-and-Fungi/Douglas-Fir

Simard, Suzanne. "How Trees Talk to Each Other." Ted.com, https://www.ted.com/talks/suzanne_simard_how_trees_talk_to_each_other

Animal Heartbeats

Langley, Liz. "The World's Weirdest Hearts for Valentine's Day." Nationalgeographic.com, 13 February 2016, https://www.nationalgeographic.com/news/2016/02/160213-animals-science-hearts-valentines-day

Specktor, Brandon. "A Blue Whale Had His Heartbeat Take for The First Time Ever." Livescience.com, Future US Inc, 26 November 2019, https://www.livescience.com/first-blue-whale-heartbeat.html

North/South Axis

Hoff, Mary. "Birds Use Their Sixth Sense to Land on Water." Audubon.org, 2 January 2014, https://www.audubon.org/magazine/birds-use-their-sixth-sense-land-water

North/South Axis (con't)

Yong, Ed. "Google Earth Shows That Cows and Deer Herds Align Like Compass Needles." Discovermagazine.com, 25 August 2008, https://www.discovermagazine.com/planet-earth/google-earth-shows-that-cow-and-deer-herds-align-like-compass-needles

MacDonald, Fiona. "Dogs Prefer to Poo Along a North–South Axis." Sciencealert.com, 10 March 2015, https://www.sciencealert.com/dogs-prefer-to-poo-along-a-north-south-axis

Size of the Universe

Cain, Fraser. "How Long Does It Take Sunlight to Reach the Earth?" Phys.org, Science X Network, 15 April 2013, https://phys.org/news/2013-04-sunlight-earth.html

Sharp, Tim. "Alpha Centauri: Closest Star to Earth." Space.com, Future US Inc., 19 January 2018, https://www.space.com/18090-alpha-centauri-nearest-star-system.html

Koberlein, Brian. "The Earth Has More Than 200 Galaxies for Each Person on Earth." Forbes.com, 13 October 2013, https://www.forbes.com/sites/briankoberlein/2016/10/13/the-universe-has-more-than-200-galaxies-for-each-person-on-earth

Math

"Donald in Mathmagic Land." Youtube.com, 1959, https://www.youtube.com/watch?v=RU5mTgZuDaE

Helmenstine, Anne Marie. "Why Mathematics is a Language." Thoughtco.com, Dotdash Publishing, 27 June 2019, https://www.thoughtco.com/why-mathematics-is-a-language-4158142

Sunflowers

Crespi, Sarah. "Why Young Sunflowers Follow the Sun." Sciencemag.org, 4 August 2016, https://www.sciencemag.org/news/2016/08/why-young-sunflowers-follow-sun

Hammers, Laurel. "Young Sunflowers Keep Time." Sciencenewsforstudents.org, 2 September 2016, https://www.sciencenewsforstudents.org/article/young-sunflowers-keep-time

Moon

Redd, Nola Taylor. "Earth's Stabilizing Moon May Unique in the Universe." Space.com, Future US Inc., 29 July 2011, https://www.space.com/12464-earth-moon-unique-solar-system-universe.html

"Moon Facts." Space-facts.com, https://space-facts.com/the-moon/

Magnetic Field

"Earth's Magnetic Field." Web.ua.es, https://web.ua.es/docivis/magnet/earths_magnetic_field2.html

"Earth's Magnetic Shield." KCTS9.pbslearningmedia.org, https://kcts9.pbslearningmedia.org/resource/nvsl.sci.space.magnetic/earths-magnetic-shield/

"How Earth Creates its Magnetic Field." Youtube.com, 2veritasium, 4 July 2018, https://www.youtube.com/watch?v=lWHxmJf6U3M

Hippos

Bradford, Alina. "Facts About Hippos." Livescience.com, Future US Inc., 1 November 2018, https://www.livescience.com/27339-hippos.html

"Hippopotamus." Nationalgeographic.com, https://www.nationalgeographic.com/ animals/mammals/h/hippopotamus/

"Hippos the Life Force of the African Rivers." Sciencedaily.com, 14 April 2015, https://www.sciencedaily.com/releases/2015/04/150414130528.htm

Light

Woodard, Chris. "Light." Explainthatstuff.com, 26 February 2020, https://www. explainthatstuff.com/light.html

"Visible Light." Science.nasa.gov, https://science.nasa.gov/ems/09_visiblelight

"Colors of Light." Sciencelearng.org.nz, Science Learning Hub, https://www.sci- encelearn.org.nz/resources/47-colours-of-light

Zimmerman, Andrew. "What is the Visible Light Spectrum?" Thoughtco.com, Dotdash Publishing, 20 February 2020, https://www.thoughtco.com/the-visible- light-spectrum-2699036

"Physics for Kids: The Science of Light Spectrum." Ducksters.com, Technological Solutions Inc., https://www.ducksters.com/science/light_spectrum.php

"Electromagnetic Spectrum." Mathisfun.com, https://www.mathsisfun.com/ physics/electromagnetic-spectrum.html

Leaves

"Learn About Leaves." Sciencewithme.com, http://www.sciencewithme.com/learn- about-leaves/

"Leaves and Leaf Anatomy." Enchantedlearning.com, https://www.enchantedlearn- ing.com/subjects/plants/leaf/

Frontal Lobe of the Human Brain

"Frontal Lobe." Academickids.com, https://academickids.com/encyclopedia/index. php/Frontal_lobe

Relationships

Lisita, Ellie. "The Four Horsemen of the Relational Apocalypse Include: Criticism, Defensiveness, Contempt, and Stonewalling." Gottman.com, 23 April 2013, https: //www.gottman.com/blog/the-four-horse-men-recognizing-criticism- contempt-defensiveness-and-stone-walling/

"Pulling Together Increases Your Pain Threshold." Sciencedaily.com, 26 September 2009, https://www.sciencedaily.com/releases/2009/09/090927150348.htm

"Re: The Work Issue." Nytimes.com, 10 March 2016, https://www.nytimes.com/ 2016/ 03/13/magazine/the-2-28-16-issue.html

Dung Beetles

"Dung Beetle." Sandiegozoo.org, https://animals.sandiegozoo.org/animals/dung-beetle

Jones, Richard. "All Praise the Humble Dung Beetle." Smithsonianmag.com, 10 January 2018, https://www.smithsonianmag.com/science-nature/the-humble- dung-beetle-180967781/

Dung Beetles (con't)

"Dung Beetle Facts." Softschools.com, https://www.softschools.com/facts/animals/dung_beetle_facts/114/

Wind

"Earth Science for Kids: Weather—Wind." Ducksters.com, Technological Solutions Inc., https://www.ducksters.com/science/earth_science/wind.php

"Wind: Air in Motion." Nationalgeographic.com, https://www.nationalgeographic.com/science/earth/earths-atmosphere/wind/

"Wind." Weatherwizkids.com, https://www.weatherwizkids.com/weather-wind.htm

Rocks

"Earth Science: Rocks and the Rock Cycle." Ducksters.com, https://www.ducksters.com/science/rocks.php

Grass

Nunez, Christina. "Grasslands Explained." Nationalgeographic.com, https://www.nationalgeographic.com/environment/habitats/grasslands/

"Grass Research." Naturalhistory.si.edu, Smithsonian Institute, https://naturalhistory.si.edu/research/botany/research/grass-research

Harris, Tom. "How Grass Works." Howstuffworks.com, https://home.howstuffworks.com/grass.htm

Love

Wu, Katherine. "Love Actually: The Science Behind Lust, Attraction, and Companionship." Harvard.edu, SITN Boston, 14 February 2019, http://sitn.hms.harvard.edu/flash/2017/love-actually-science-behind-lust-attraction-companionship/

"Science of Love." BBC.co.uk, https://www.bbc.co.uk/science/hottopics/love/

Greenberg, Melanie. "The Science of Love and Attachment." Psychologytoday.com, Sussex Publishers Inc., 30 March 2016, https://www.psychologytoday.com/us/blog/the-mindful-self-express/201603/the-science-love-and-attachment

Soil

"Earth Science for Kids: Soil." Ducksters.com, Technological Solutions Inc., https://www.ducksters.com/science/earth_science/soil_science.php

"What is Soil?" Soils4kids.org, Soil Science Society of America, https://www.soils4kids.org/about

Desert

Nunez, Christina. "Desserts Explained." Nationalgeographic.com, https://www.nationalgeographic.com/environment/habitats/deserts/

"Dessert." Nationalgeographic.org, https://www.nationalgeographic.org/encyclopedia/desert/

Sand

"Learn About Sand." Britannica.com, https://www.britannica.com/video/185632/formation-sand-quartz-role-processes-weathering-grains

Sand (con't)

"How Does Sand Form." Oceanservice.noaa.gov, https://oceanservice.noaa.gov/facts/sand.html

Castro, Joseph. "What is Sand?" Livescience.com, 28 March 2013, https://www.livescience.com/34748-what-is-sand-beach-sand.html

Plant Communication

Karban, Richard. "Can Plants Talk to Each Other?" Youtube.com, TedEd, 2 May 2016, https://www.youtube.com/watch?v=xOXSqy05EO0

Grant, Bonnie L. "Can Plants Talk to Each Other—What Do They Use to Communicate?" Gardeningknowhow.com, https://www.gardeningknowhow.com/garden-how-to/info/can-plants-talk-to-each-other.htm

"Plants Talk to Each Other to Determine Growth." Earth.com, 2 May 2018, https://www.earth.com/news/plants-talk-soil-growth/

Hummingbirds

Penninsi, Elizabeth. "High Speed Cameras Reveal How Hummingbirds Turn on a Dime." Sciencemag.org, 8 February 2018, https://www.sciencemag.org/news/2018/02/high-speed-cameras-reveal-how-hummingbirds-can-turn-dime

"The Hummingbird Wing Beat Challenge." Audubon.org, 22 April 2020, https://www.audubon.org/news/the-hummingbird-wing-beat-challenge

Rico-Guevara, Alejandro. "The Hummingbird Tongue is a Fluid Trap, not a Capillary Tube." PNAS.org, 7 June 2011, https://www.pnas.org/content/108/23/9356

Giving

Suttie, Jill. "5 Ways Giving is Good for You." Greatergoodberkley.edu, 13 December 2010, https://greatergood.berkeley.edu/article/item/5_ways_giving_is_good_for_you

About the Author
and Illustrator

Tonia and Kory live in Seattle with their three daughters. One of their great passions is serving together in prayer ministries at their church—a place that encourages creative expressions of faith.

Tonia works as a marriage and family therapist, and Kory works as a creative director. Their professional careers, along with their love of the outdoors, have shaped how they see the presence of God. Together with their three daughters, they often explore one of the many Pacific Northwest waterways via their stand-up paddle boards.

@tonia.l.davidson

rehabgraphics.com

Made in the USA
Monee, IL
29 April 2021